Art Therapy for ASD Students in Schools

15 Creative Group Activities to Build Connection and Emotional Expression

Lyndsey Hedger

ATR-BC, LCPC

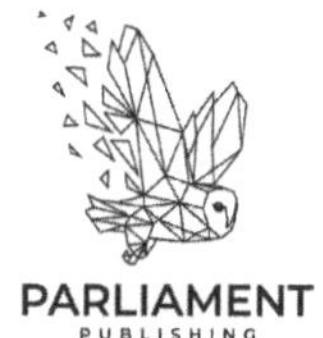

PARLIAMENT
PUBLISHING

Published by:

Parliament Publishing

For rights and permissions inquiries, please contact:

Parliament Publishing

info@theparliamentgroup.com

First Edition: 2025

The information contained in this book is for educational and informational purposes only. The author and publisher make no guarantees regarding the effectiveness of the techniques described and assume no liability for any outcomes resulting from their application.

Printed in the United States of America.

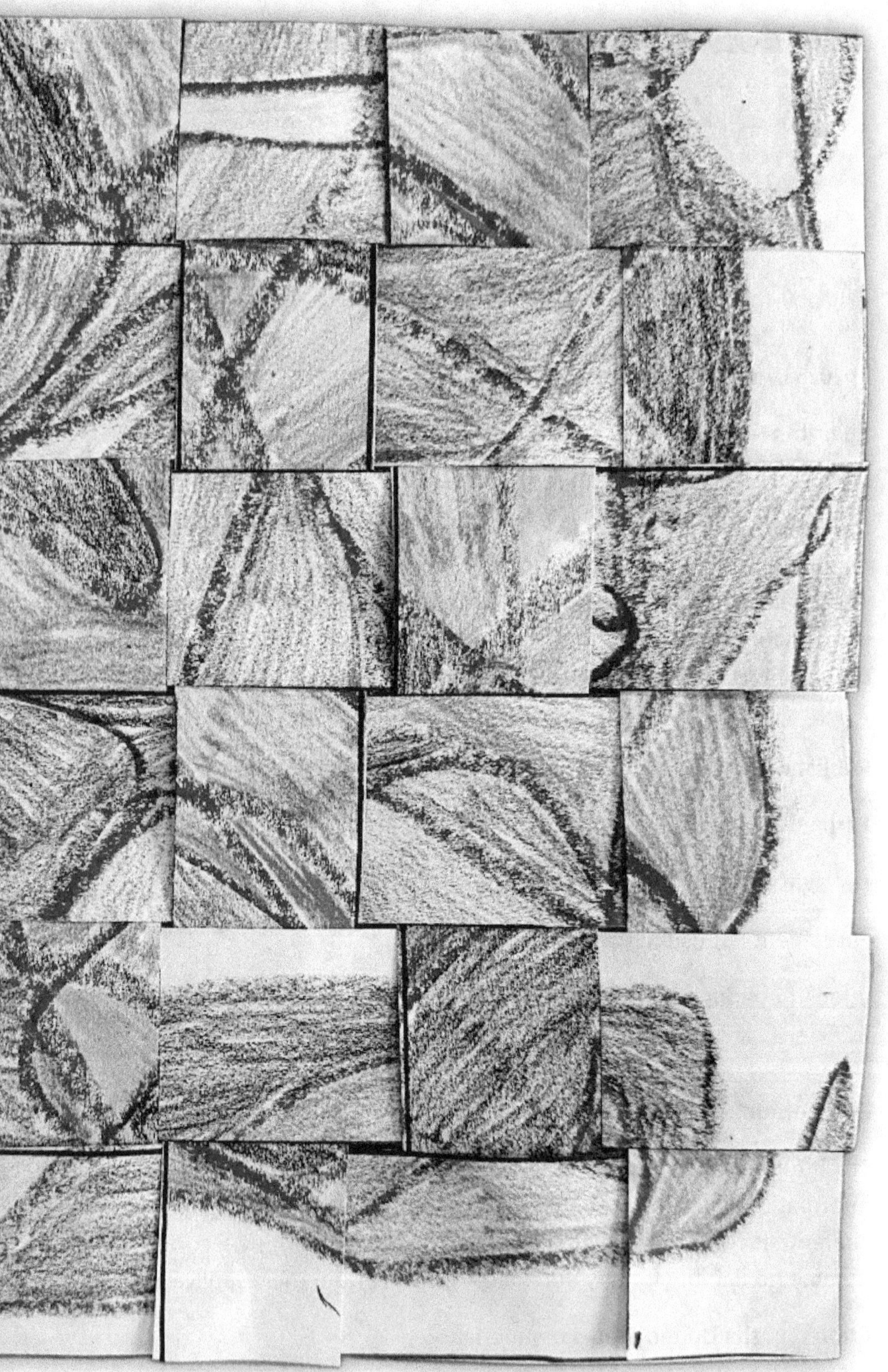

Lyndsey Hedger is an outstanding art therapist and has extensive experience working with the Autistic community. I am fortunate to have worked with her and have seen how her art therapy interventions positively impact clients and allow a space for them to safely explore experiences through art making. This book provides outlets for clients to use creativity and flexibility to express their internal experiences. The field of art therapy is lucky to have her!

- **Kelly Dunne, Psy.D.**

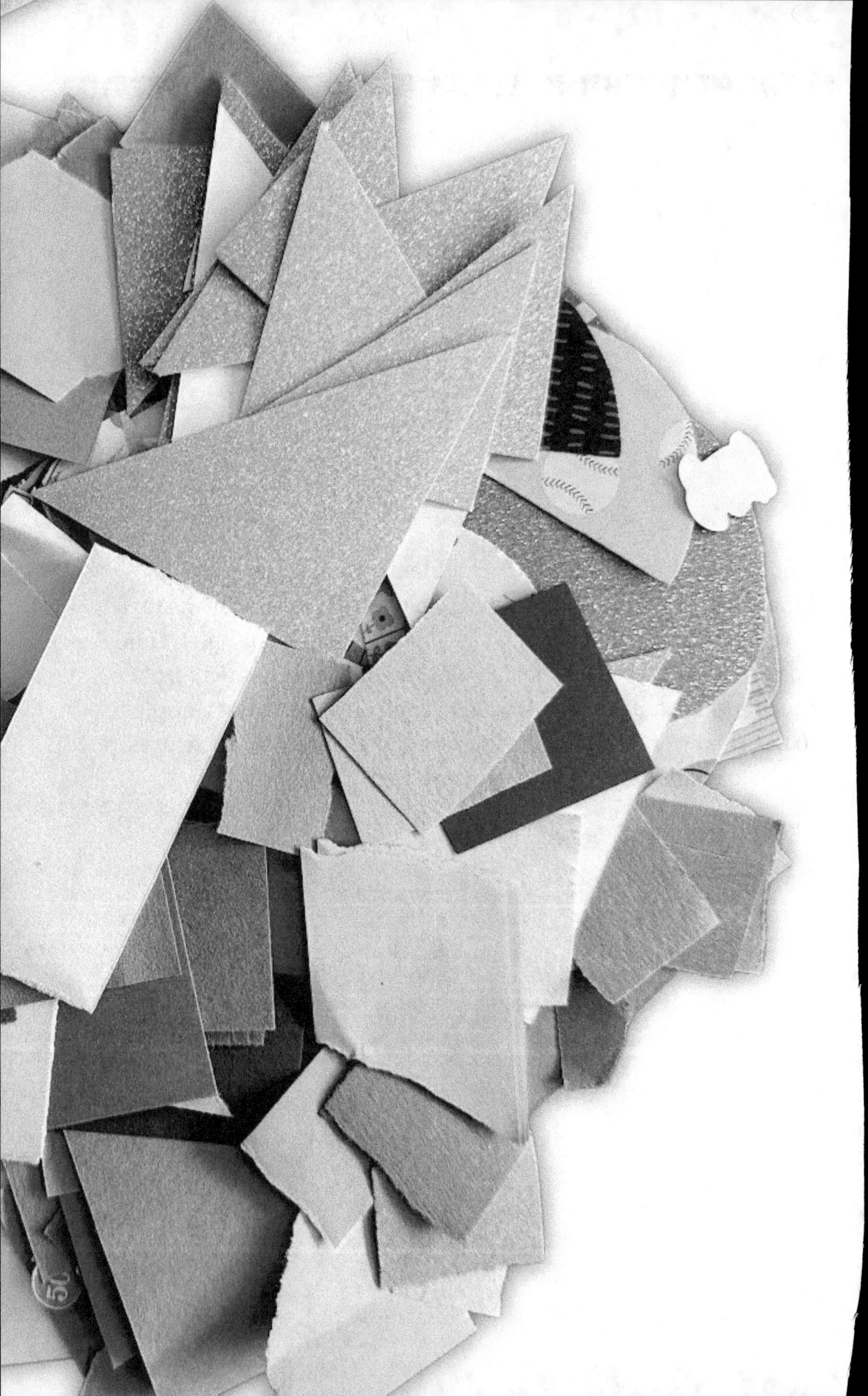

Table of Contents

Introduction

As an art therapist working primarily with level one autistic students in a therapeutic day school setting, I have seen firsthand the power of art therapy through weekly group sessions. Research has shown that art therapy is an incredibly effective modality to support ASD individuals who may have difficulty with executive functioning, social skills, flexibility, and sensory regulation, to name a few (Durrani, 2019). Further, there is limited art therapy research to show that art as an intervention with clients with ASD can contribute to increasing overall mood, interaction with others, flexibility, appropriate expression of emotion, and problem-solving skills, and can decrease behavioral challenges, rigidity, and emotional dysregulation (Schweizer, C. et al., 2017; Schweizer, C. et al., 2019). This book does not aim to treat autism or "fix" autism. Rather, it aims to provide a way for students to discover themselves and explore themes within and around them to make meaning. Art therapy provides an effective method for practitioners when talk therapy may fall short.

The purpose of this book is to provide a starting point for creating a semester-long curriculum for an art therapy group inside a school. A credentialed art therapist has led each of these directives with school-age ASD students varying from 7 years - 22 years old, with modifications when necessary. The groups that these directives were modeled for were 10 students; however, they are all easily sized up or down as needed. As you move through this book, each directive will explain the benefits and importance of the activity for autistic students. As mentioned, this book is primarily based on the author's work with Level 1 ASD individuals, who typically have emotional and behavioral concerns along with comorbid mental health difficulties. However, with modifications, most directives can still be effective for Level 2 and even Level 3 students.

Before we dive into these (super) fun directives, I want to cover a few disclaimers. In order for these directives to be used safely and effectively, firstly ensure that all materials that are being implemented are safe for your specific population. If you are not sure of the safety of scissors, for example, tear instead of cut or pre-cut the items that will need to be used. Secondly, using a trauma-informed lens, make sure that images being used or the themes being used will not unnecessarily trigger your clients. Thirdly, the space in which you lead these directives should promote safety, sustainability, and comfortability so that as exploration and expression occurs, students may feel empowered to create! (Danieli, Y. et al., 2019).

Disclaimer:

These directives have been planned and implemented by a credentialed art therapist. If you are not an art therapist and wish to use pieces of these directives or the entirety of the directive, please ensure you are working in collaboration with an art therapist in order to work within the scope of your profession. While I do not believe that you must be an art therapist to use art in your practice (whether in a group or individual setting), it must be used with utmost caution and again, with support from an art therapist to ensure safety, proper administration, and correct use of materials. It should be noted that at the end of the book, included with references, is a list of art therapy resources for your use.

Sensory Sketchbooks

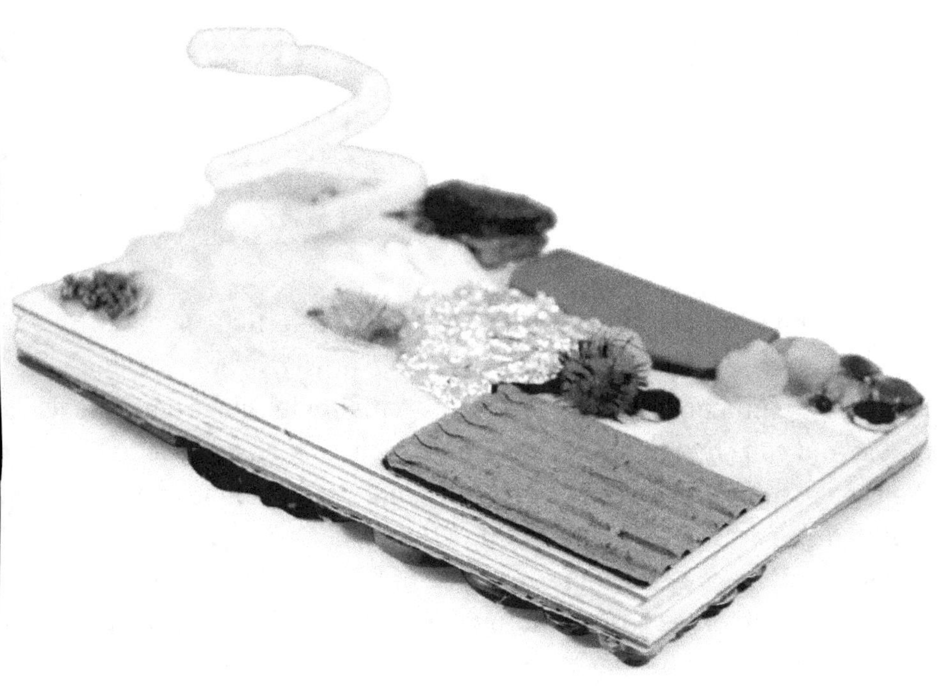

Materials Needed

Paper

Mat board cut to size

Glue

Puff balls, pipe cleaners, sensory strips, google eyes, cardboard, foam, sequins, etc.

Ruler

Bone folder (or similar)

Bookmaking is my favorite type of artmaking and getting to share one of these processes with my students is a privilege. Bookmaking provides an intimate work of art that conceals some things and reveals others and can create a moment in time that students can use to honor their experience and their story. Additionally, getting to make a book that doubles as a fidget is just short of a dream! I have gotten quite accustomed to always having some type of fidget within arm's reach, and being able to lead my groups through making a book that also gives them sensory input when needed makes this a significant directive.

This accordion book project can be completed in one to two 40-minute group sessions. I have successfully led this directive with ages 8-21! It is a great directive for students who may not consider themselves "good" at art, and can also be a great regulating activity for students who need significant sensory input. The end result is an accordion book that will allow for mark making on the front and the back of paper. This type of book also works well for gluing items into it because instead of fanning out as a normal book would, it can contain the items due to the style of the folds. The covers provide a fidget for students (soft or rough or both), can create music (foil, google eyes, etc.), and provide each of these in a quieter manner so that it is not a distraction if they're using it at a later time in their classes. These fidget books are one of a kind and students are sure to love the process AND the product!

Before beginning this activity with your group, there are some preparations for this book project. If your students are more advanced, or if you are choosing to do this with adults then you could have them complete the prep, but it will likely add one session to this project.

For safety considerations, cut everything down to size (materials for front of covers included) before group so that no sharp items are needed for this activity.

Group Leader Prep:

1. Decide what size books you would like your group to create. The book these instructions reflect is 4x6". It can be sized up or down depending on needs of the group, as well as cost of materials. You will need two pieces for each student.

2. Once size is chosen, using an Xacto knife or a paper cutter, cut down either mat board or book board to (for this book) 4.25x6.25". You want the book covers to be slightly larger than your text block inside the book. Once cut, set them aside for group.

3. For the text block, I recommend large drawing paper (18x24") so that you have enough paper for the folds required in the accordion book.

4. Using either your Xacto or paper cutter, you will cut down your paper so that it measures 6x24". It should look like a very long strip of paper. Using these measurements you should be able to get three strips from the paper.

5. For your group, you will now have one strip of paper per person, as well as two book covers per person. Additionally, I like to gather all of the sensory related items that will be glued on the cover before the group begins. However, you could also have students choose them during the group.

Group Instructions:

1. Students will receive their two book covers to begin. Once they have them, they will choose any items (that are gluable) they would like and place them on their covers.
2. Items can include cardboard strips, foam, puff balls, google eyes, sequins, etc.
3. If students want heavier objects on their covers, consider assisting them with hot gluing the items, if suitable.
4. Once students have chosen their items for the cover, they will glue them on using Elmer's white glue or a glue stick (or hot glue, if appropriate).
5. After all items are glued, the covers can be set aside to dry. MAKE SURE NAMES ARE ON THE COVERS!
6. At this point, I encourage students to look around their area to make sure there is no glue or extra cover items that will ruin their or their peers' paper.

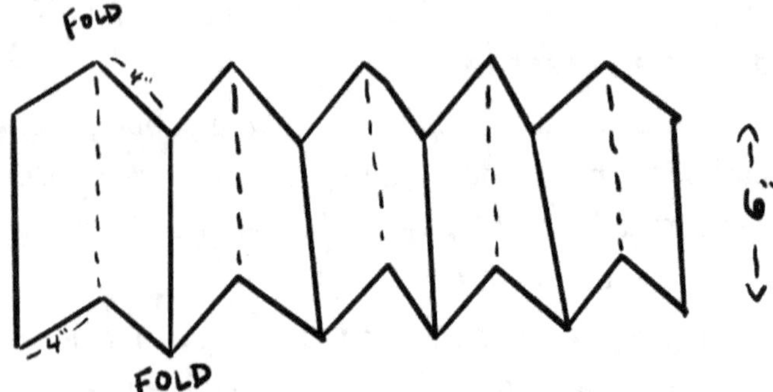

7. Now, they will receive their strip of paper, and using a ruler they will mark a line at 4" from the edge of their paper. If students may have difficulty with this, leader can pre-mark the line or assist during the group.
8. After one line has been drawn, they will fold on the line so that the first fold is at 4". I have students use bone folders for this. A bone folder allows a nice, crisp line by scoring on the fold. If bone folders are not available, consider a spoon or fingernail to crisp the line.

9. Now, and this is where some students may have difficulty, they will begin the accordion fold. Using the first 4" line for reference, each additional fold will also be made to be in line with the first fold.

10. As they fold, it is folded on the front, then on the back, etc. If this is still confusing, I remind students they want to create mountains and valleys as they fold. (see image for reference)

11. Once the folding is complete, the student will have a text block measuring approximately 4x6" and two decorated book covers measuring just slightly over 4x6".

12. Students will take one end of the folded paper and glue it to the inside of the first cover. Use the bone folder or replacement tool to adhere the paper to the cover.

13. Lastly, students will repeat this process for the back end of the paper to the inside of the second cover.

14. If there is time, students can begin drawing in their sketchbooks, however this stage of the project is optional!

Modifications/Autism Considerations:

1. For younger students or Level 2-3 ASD students, choose and divide items for covers into bags for them that are provided at the beginning of the group.

2. Pre-fold the first fold or all folds for the students. It should be noted, if all folds are pre-folded, this activity could be completed in one 40-minute group.

3. As mentioned, a hot glue gun could be used for heavier or more finicky objects (i.e. pipe cleaners, small stones) but please ensure a group leader or aid is able to supervise or complete this step for students.

Example

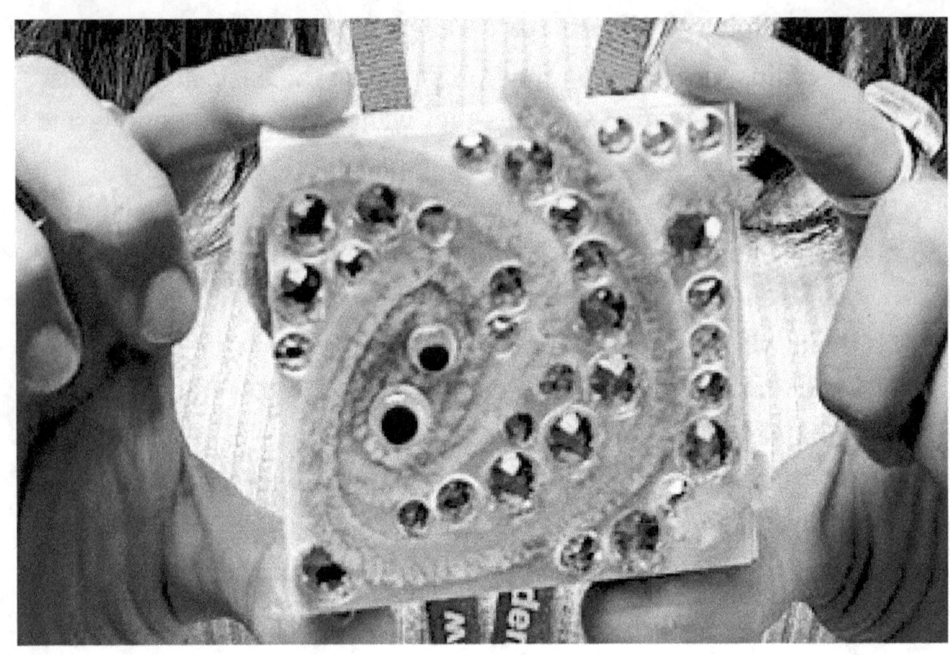

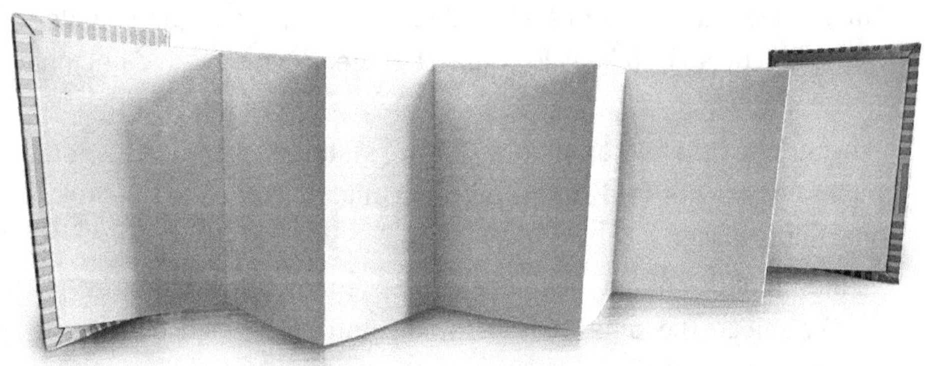

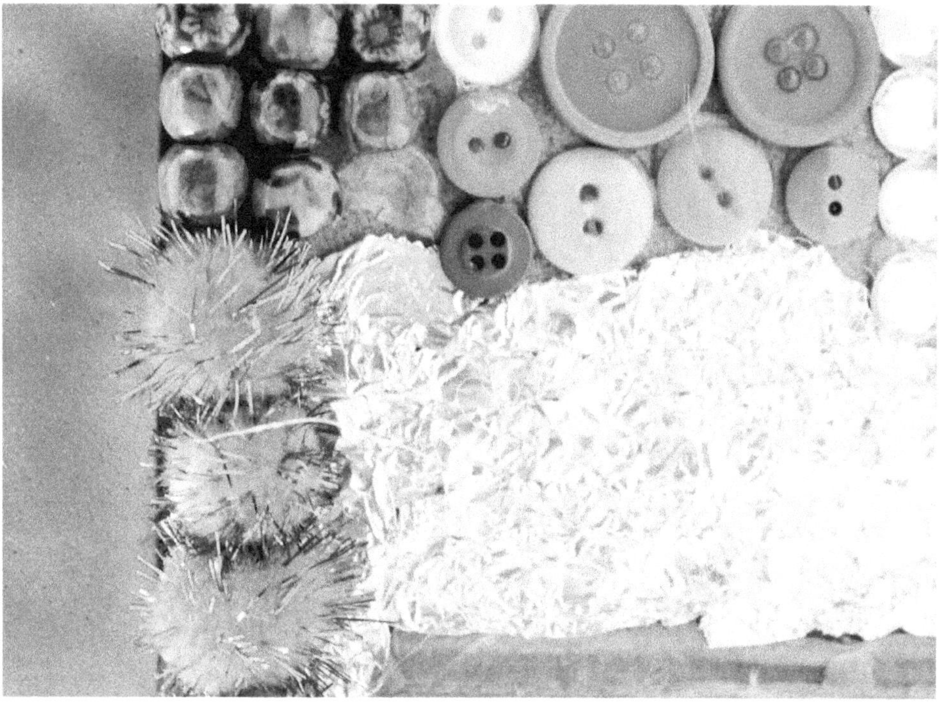

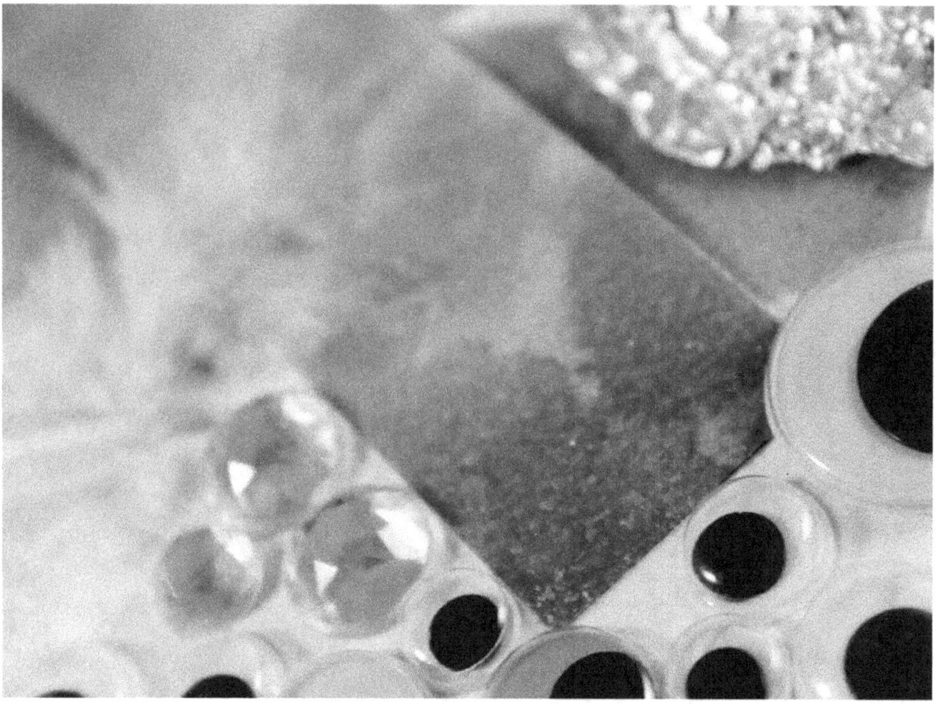

DIRECTIVE 2

Mystery Mash Up!

(Adjective, Noun, In the Style of)

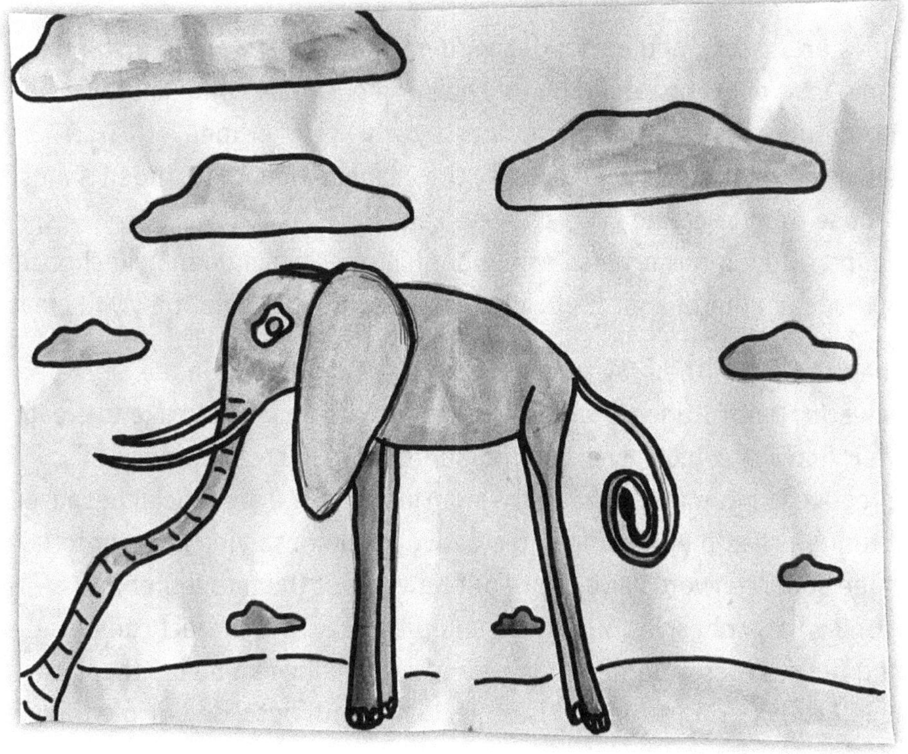

Colorful Elephant in the Style of Salvador Dali

Materials Needed

Paper

Drawing utensils (crayons, markers, colored pencils, etc.)

Art History reference
(see group leader prep)

I love art history, and in working with my students, I want to instill that same love of art history in them. This project can be completed in one 40-minute session, and can be done by any age of students (8-17). This activity uses three lists, created by the group leader, that students must choose from to create their artwork. Each list is as follows: adjectives, nouns, and famous artists throughout history. Each student will choose one of each out of a jar that will give the outline for what they will create.

The drawing on the previous page is "Colorful Elephant in the Style of Salvador Dali." Students can use any materials they would like to create their drawing, which gives back some freedom in creating since this directive is more restricted in theme. This project is beneficial because it requires flexible thinking and creative problem solving in order to take three separate words and figure out how to put them together into a (somewhat) cohesive composition. Additionally, this project can be silly and fun to teach students that art and art making can be lighthearted. When considering autism, this project is helpful because flexible thinking can be a struggle for a lot of students. This project can allow for this skill to be honed and their flexibility be stretched in a way that is not daunting. It can also give students a project in which perfection is not on the forefront. In my experience, ASD individuals can have difficulty when things do not turn out perfectly, or as expected. Because this project is a chosen theme, they may not have preconceived notions of what to expect - this can give freedom to explore.

For safety considerations, this project is an excellent choice based on material usage because any materials, even crayons or Crayola markers, can be used to create a unique artwork. One caution is to be sure any artworks or artists that students may be choosing are appropriate for the age and developmental level of the students. I choose a list of artists (and recommended artworks) for my students before group, not only to ensure appropriateness for students, but also for appropriateness for a school. Depending on your setting, there could of course be more leeway for this.

Group Leader Prep:

1. Type or write out three separate lists of common adjectives, nouns, and famous artists respectively (I've included my lists here)

Adjectives	**Nouns**	**Artists**
• Happy	• Milkshake	• Monet
• Colorful	• Elephant	• Van Gogh
• Silly	• Schoolhouse	• Seurat
• Sad	• Stadium	• Munch
• Grumpy	• Baseball	• Warhol
• Beautiful	• Cloud	• Braque
• Bumpy	• Phone	• Kahlo
• Spiky	• Guitar	• Picasso

2. In order to give suggestions for what type of marks should be made for each artist that may be chosen, I compile a chart for my students that includes all possible artists that they could pick for their drawing. I have included a couple to give an example (see on the following page), however I include every artist from the list on the chart.

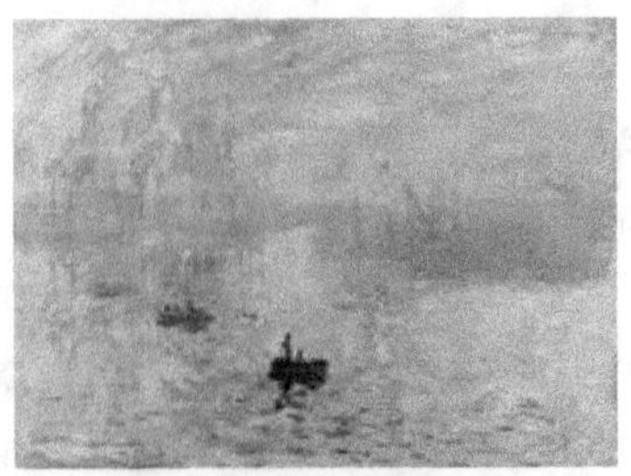

Claude Monet, *Impressionism*

- Unblended color
- Bare impression of form
- Small brush strokes
- Emphasis on natural depiction of light

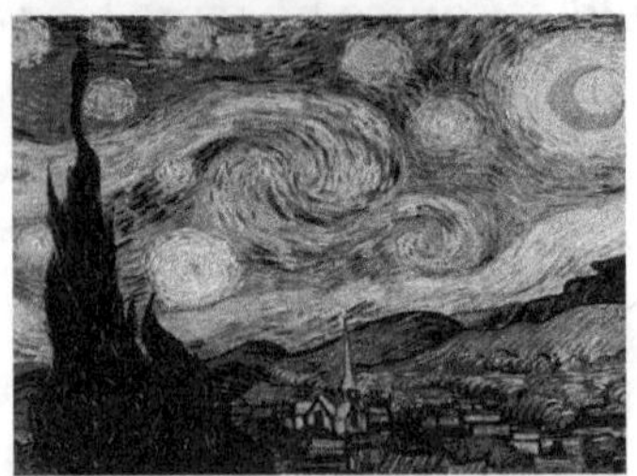

Vincent Van Gogh, *Post Impressionism*

- Vivid colors
- Thick application of paint
- Distorted forms
- Geometric shapes

3. For the chart of art history blurbs, make one to two copies and laminate to have available for students. You could also create a slideshow if possible.

4. Take your three lists and cut each word on each list into small strips and fold them.

5. Using either bags or jars, separate the strips of paper into each of their respective lists and place in three separate bags or jars.

Group Instructions

1. Each student will get one piece of paper (I use 9x12", but any size will work) and a pencil.

2. Pass around, or have students come up to the group leader, to choose the three groupings of paper strips with nouns, adjectives, and artists.

3. Once each student has one of each, I have the student state out loud what they will be drawing. I've found this helps the prompt become more salient for students.

4. Point students to laminated copies of artist blurbs and answer any questions they may have.

5. Student will then choose materials to begin drawing. I recommend they draw with pencil first and then outline or color in their drawing with their chosen materials.

6. Title drawing with this format: Adjective, Noun, In the Style Of

7. If time allows and if students would like to, have each student share their artwork and title.

Modifications/Autism Considerations

1. If students have difficulty with the rigidity of only one choice, you can allow them one extra pick from a jar. It should be noted that once the second pick is made, there cannot be another switch!

2. Consider giving fewer options for materials if your group has difficulty with too broad of options.

3. At times I have found that students may struggle with drawing. For particularly younger students, I offer Model Magic as a substitute for paper and pencil.

4. If you would like to take this project a step further, you can also create a list of artists that reflect diversity, including but not limited to artists of color, women artists, international artists, etc.

A Note

When running my groups, my utmost hope is for students to be able to step outside of their comfort zone when they are ready. If I know a student is capable, I will push them to stay inside the bounds of what I have offered for the directive. However, if I know that a student's self-esteem or excitement for art therapy may be hindered, then I will meet them where they are to help support a positive experience and an art piece they can be proud of!

Example

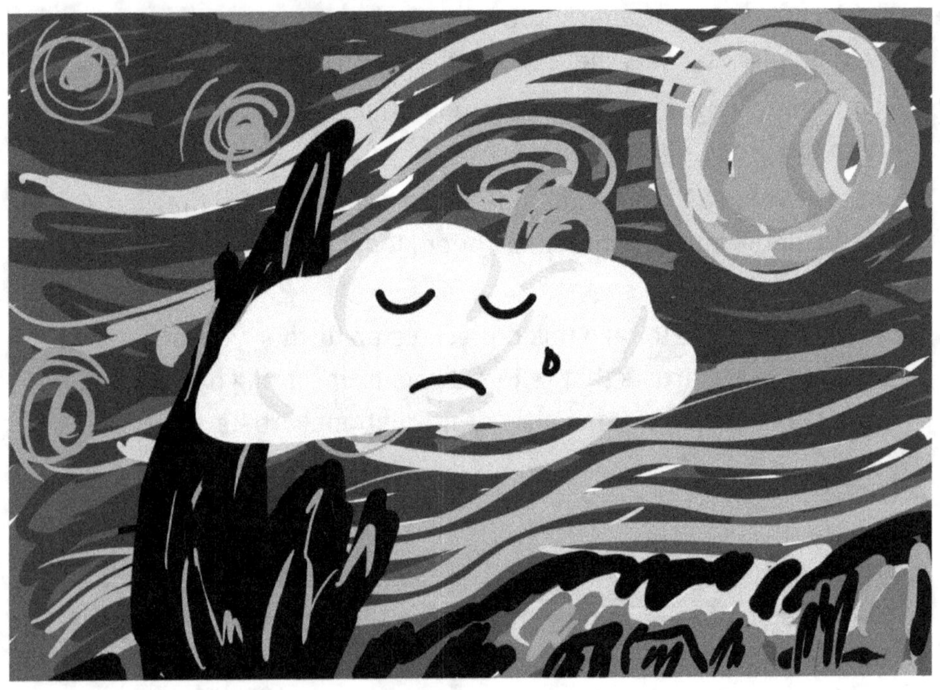

Sad Cloud in the Style of Van Gogh

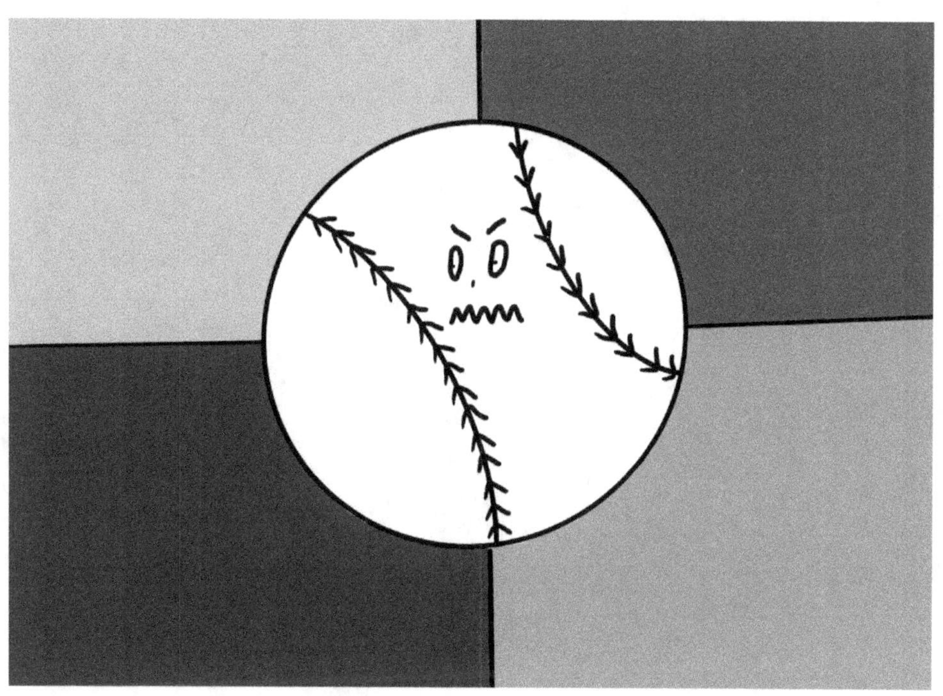

Angry Baseball in the Style of Warhol

DIRECTIVE 3

Scribble Weaving

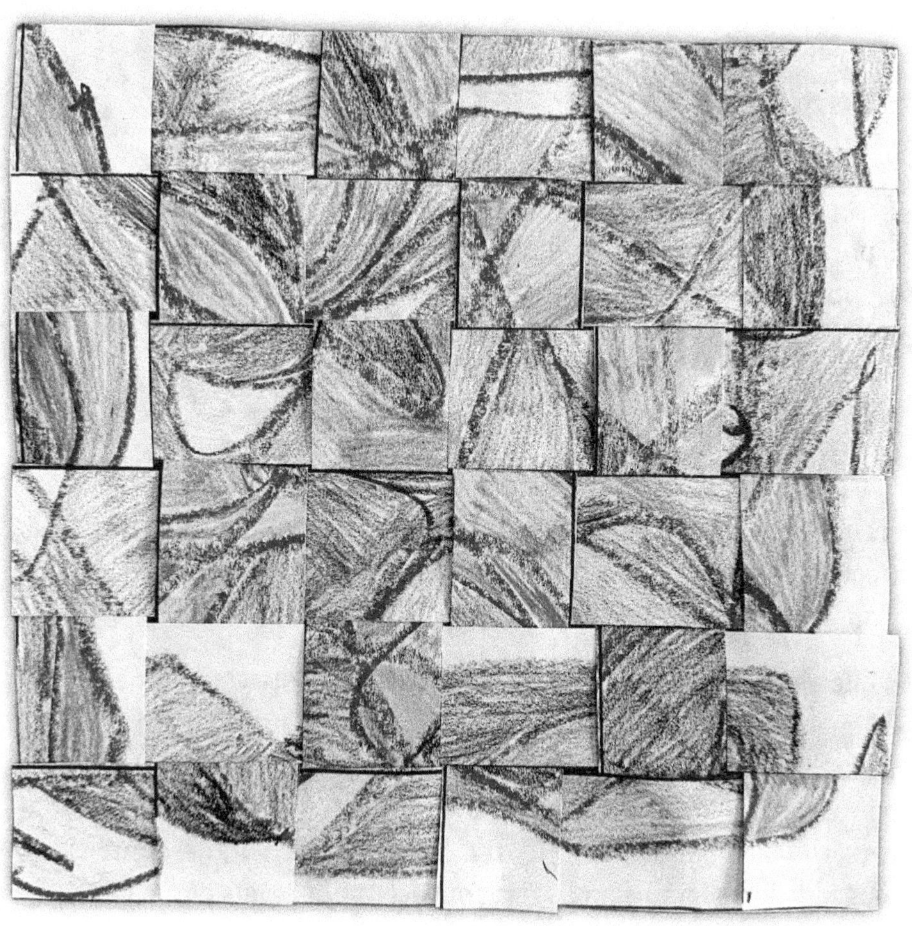

Materials Needed

Paper

Oil Pastels

Sharpies

Scotch tape

Scissors

"Expressive Therapies Continuum" has provided art therapists a model for supporting clients through the creative level (cognitive and symbolic, perceptual and affective, kinesthetic and sensory) with appropriate materials and directives to lead them through each of these components (Hinz, L.D., 2009).

This activity allows for ASD students to experience a kinesthetic activity through sensory input and then move to the perceptual level through an affective portion of the activity and finally to the cognitive level through symbolism.

By allowing opportunity for a traditional scribble drawing, students will engage in large movements and get loosened up for creative mark making. Then they will find symbols and imagery throughout their scribble and outline them. Finally, they will cut the drawing into even strips and plan out a pattern for their weaving. Each of these three steps highlights important aspects of each of the levels of the ETC with creativity running through the entire process. I find the benefits of this hugely important for ASD students, and include large movements and the sensory input that accompanies, finding highlighted moments within their drawing and the processing/organization of the perceptual level, and finally, planning and implementing through problem solving. Inherent in these processes is opportunity to progress in executive functioning, exploration through color and symbolism, and fine motor skills, to name only a few.

This project typically takes two 40-minute art therapy group sessions, with the first being the scribble and find portion and the second being the weaving portion. For younger students, I recommend cutting the strips for them and assisting with the weaving, but for older students they can likely handle the strip cutting independently. Either way, this directive is appropriate for all ages, but works best with students 8-15, in my experience. Some safety considerations include making sure students in your group can handle scissors safely as they are needed to cut strips of the scribble drawing needed for the final weaving portion. If students cannot be safe with regular scissors, consider using safety scissors. If this is still a concern, they can tear the strips once they are scored, but just know that the strips may not be torn evenly. However, the idea of planning out and implementing the weaving will still be salient.

Group Leader Prep

1. Prepare sheets of paper measured around 11x14". This will give enough room to create a large scribble and strips for the weaving.
2. Ensure oil pastels and markers are available for use.
3. For a modification, group leader can measure out where the strips will need to be cut. For this directive, the strips are 1" wide. Group leader could use a Sharpie before group begins and draw out the lines for students. This is up to leader discretion on ability levels of group.

Instructions

1. Group leader should set a timer for 30 seconds. Student will choose one oil pastel color and begin scribbling. Group leader should remind students to use large arm movements!
2. Once the 30 seconds is over, students should put down their pastel and the scribble portion is complete.

3. Then students will choose a different color marker and they will spend the next 15-30 minutes finding shapes, patterns, lines, etc in their scribbles. Once they find them, they will use their marker and outline the shapes they see. This portion could take the rest of group, or students might move relatively quickly through this part.

4. Once all students have completed this previous step, they will get a ruler and a Sharpie and they will measure 1" lines from edge to edge of their paper.

5. After all lines have been drawn, the students will use scissors and cut on the lines they created to make the strips. Make sure if students are sitting at a table, they keep their pile of strips separate from their peers.

6. Students will begin weaving by laying half of their strips vertically in front of them. It helps to tape the topmost edge of each strip onto the table.

7. Then, student will begin using their other half of strips and begin weaving them into the existing strips by going under one and over, under and over, until it reaches the end of the strips. Like this image:

8. This method will be repeated until the remaining strips are gone. If the student begins under with their first strip, they will then go over to begin the next one.

9. Once the weaving process is complete, students can choose to tape their strips together to ensure they do not fall out of the pattern.

Modifications/Autism Considerations

1. This project can be simplified if students are having difficulty with the full set of processes.
2. The group leader can choose to draw the lines before group begins to remove a step of the process.
3. Instead of cutting the strips, students can tear the strips.
4. If students are unable to manage the weaving without support, group leader and/or co leader can help get them started.
5. I also recommend having a visual reminder of over, under, over, under, etc for students to refer to.
6. If Sharpies are a concern, use a black colored pencil or marker instead.

Example

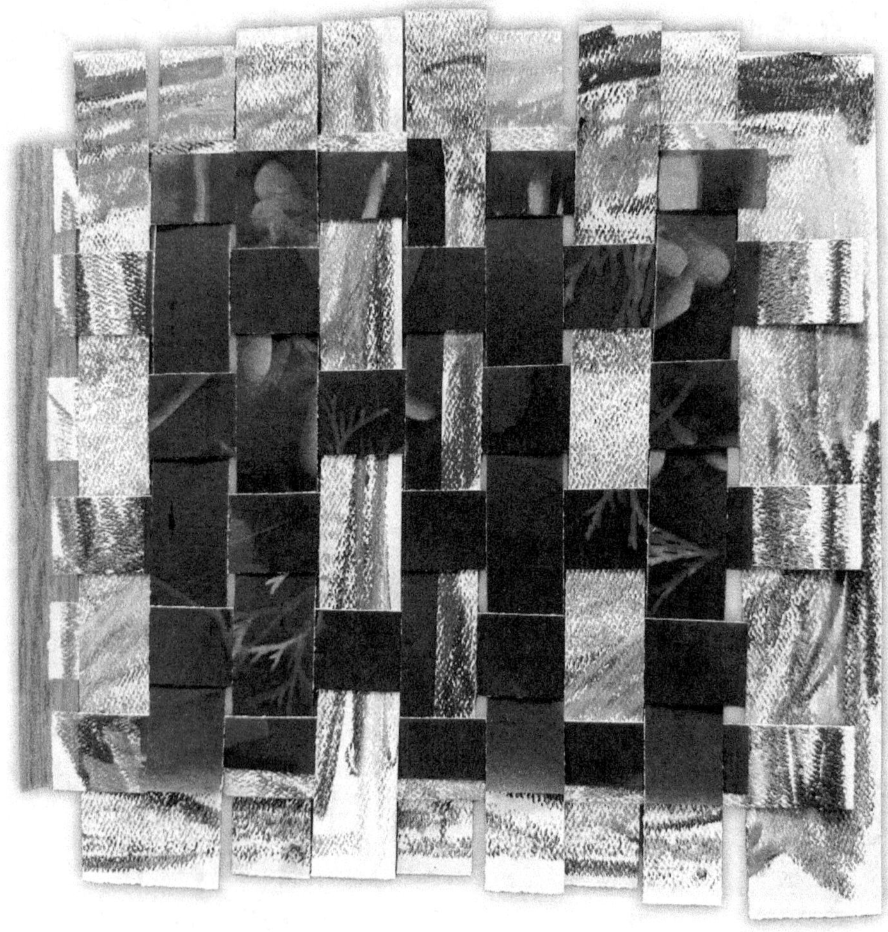

Model Magic/Clay Strength Animals

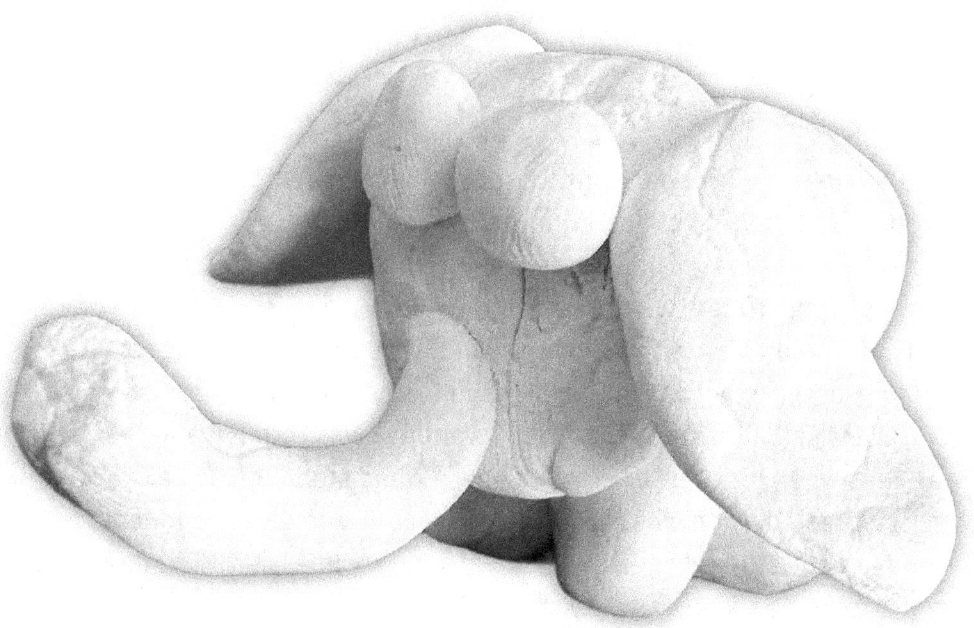

Materials Needed

Model Magic (or air-dry clay)

Acrylic paint

Paint brushes

Newspaper

Crayola markers

I will be honest. Clay and sculptures, in general, were never my forte through art school or even now in my own studio practice. However, I love this activity because my students love this activity. Getting to lead art therapy groups where we use clay and Model Magic are my favorite days. ASD individuals often thrive when given the opportunity to engage in a sensory laden activity. Clay offers this in a way that few other mediums can. Likewise, when students may view themselves through a negative self-lens when it comes to drawing, these same students may discover an artistic breakthrough when using clay or Model Magic. I have found that some autistic students see the world around them easier when modeling in 3D modalities, whereas they may struggle to create something within a flat surface. When I present this activity, I immediately offer either clay or Model Magic. While some students love the feeling of wet, air-dry clay on their hands, others want no part of it. If this is the case, I provide Model Magic instead. This project is fairly straightforward and gives students a great opportunity to look inward and then express themselves outward in a non threatening way.

This project is completed over two 40-minute art therapy groups and is an accessible project for all ages and all ability levels. There is no prep needed before group for the leader, assuming that clay and Model Magic are readily available in your studio or classroom. Students will be instructed to think of an animal that has attributes that they admire or would like to emulate, or maybe already emulate. It can be as simple as running fast or can be deeper, such as being in a pack or having a good memory. I leave it up to the students, as this project can be a great entry point for students buying into art therapy. One benefit of this project is that at times students may have some difficulty coming up with an attribute they see in themselves or that they would like to see, and this gives peers around them an opportunity to show belonging and give them an answer they may not have thought of. Another incredible benefit is allowing students a way to come up with an idea in the abstract and see it come to life all in just a few moments. Once students have their animal in mind, they will sculpt it with clay or Model Magic. The following week they can paint their clay animals! This experience offers students a moment of exploration within themselves and then they get to choose what parts of that exploration they would like to share through the expression of 3D art.

Safety is also a minimal concern with this project! Though students could have access to clay modeling tools, it is not at all a requirement. They can use water to smooth clay and their fingers to mold as they see fit. For Model Magic, no tools are required. With the lack of safety concerns, this is an added benefit for this directive.

Group Instructions

1. Students will brainstorm and choose an animal that they admire, that they see themselves in, that they would like to emulate, or that they like characteristics of.
2. If preferred, students can sketch out their animal on a scratch sheet of paper.
3. After choosing their animal, students will select either air-dry clay or Model Magic and begin sculpting their animal.
4. If available, students may choose to use clay modeling tools to add texture, and water to smooth out clay.

5. Once the student completes their animal, I recommend carving their initials in the bottom of the animal, or placing it on a piece of cardboard with their name next to their animal.

6. Once the clay or Model Magic has dried—likely by the next session—students will select three paint colors to add detail to their animal.

Modifications/Autism Considerations

1. If students have difficulty visualizing their animal consider printing off a photo of the animal for reference.

2. Students may have difficulty choosing an animal and if this occurs, I widen the prompt to include characters that students may see in preferred shows or games.

3. If students want to use clay rather than Model Magic, but do not like the feeling of the clay, you can offer them gloves while working with the clay.

Example

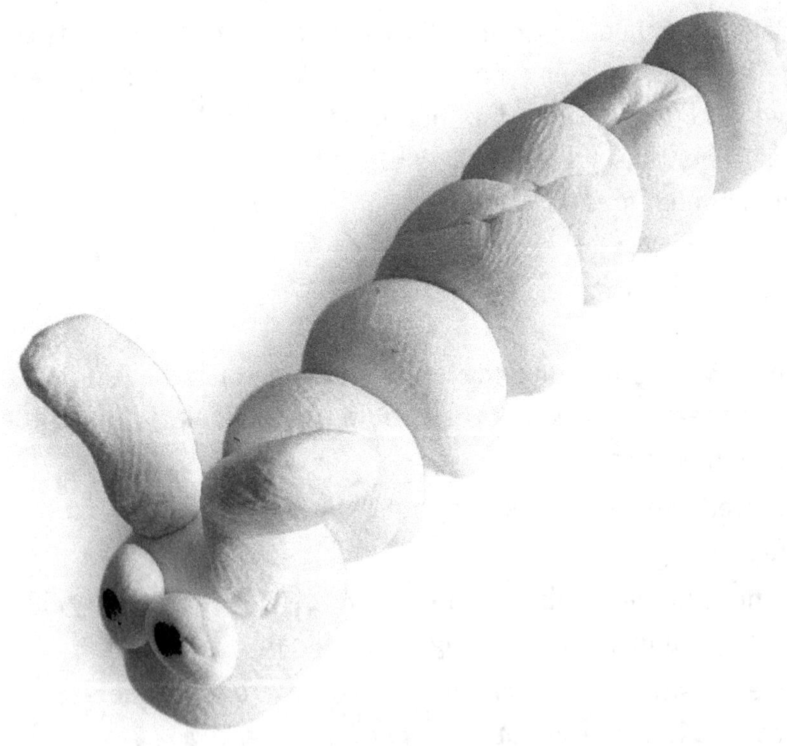

DIRECTIVE 5

Styrofoam Printmaking

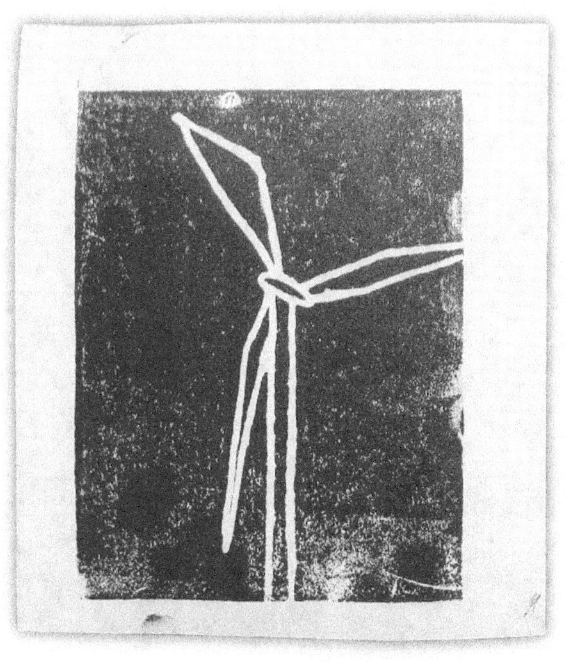

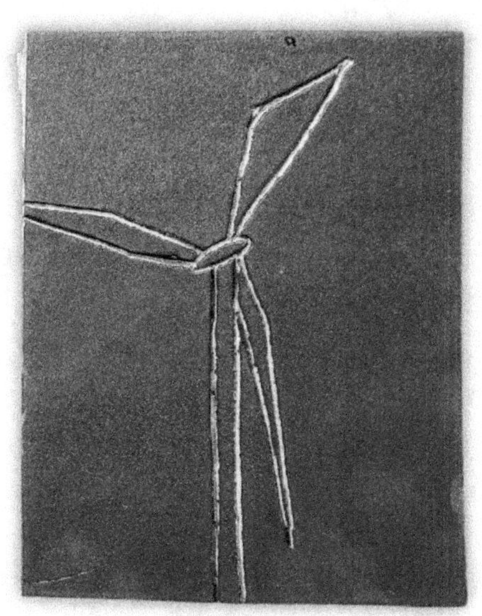

Materials Needed

Small styrofoam plates

Paper, cut to same size as
plates

Pencils and pens

Water-based relief ink

Plexiglass

Plastic spoons

Printmaking brayers

Either a:

Intaglio press

Handheld barren
(burnisher)

Or a metal spoon

Ah, printmaking! My first love in the art world, and one that I love
teaching my students as they get to witness a small drawing turn into
a creation of art again and again! I love teaching printmaking in my art
therapy groups because it feels like fine art, and for my students who do
not have a traditional art class and who do not have a traditional district
school, it is an opportunity for them to engage in a centuries old art
practice! This project is beneficial for so many reasons, but why I think
this is worth your time to lead in an art therapy group is that it teaches
executive functioning and helps support autistic students' ability to
follow directions.

This is one of my few directives that takes multiple weeks to complete and that requires specific and sequential steps in order to be successful. Because of this facet of printmaking, it allows me to teach accepting mistakes and happy accidents that occur constantly in printmaking. For ASD students each of these benefits can also be incredibly difficult to accept and adhere to.

This is where the therapy enters in so naturally and creates a space where I can support as they learn and explore. And the majority of the time, students are thrilled with at least one of their prints and the self-esteem they build through this process is a joy to behold.

This printmaking directive is a relief printmaking method, meaning that the students carve into a block and what is carved away will be white, and what is left will be colored. This relief printmaking project involves students first drawing a sketch on a small, 4x6" piece of paper and then transferring it to their "matrix". A matrix in printmaking is the block or surface that will be printed from once inked up and burnished. The matrix, in this case, is a styrofoam print plate. These are very reasonably priced on Amazon, and you can typically go to your local grocery store and get FREE styrofoam meat plates (without the meat of course). Once they have their matrix with their design on it, they will ink it up with water-based inks and then burnish onto paper to complete the process. I find that students sometimes have a difficult time seeing the end result in their minds - I implore them to trust the process and watch the magic of printmaking happen! I also typically require students to do at least two prints from their one matrix so that the understanding of how multiples work in printmaking becomes clear.

This project does require planning, hence the executive functioning we are all going to improve in, and does require at least two 40-minute sessions, but I have found that three sessions is the sweet spot for students to carefully plan and implement this project. I have done this directive with students as young as eight; however, with a group of around 10 students, it works best with ages 12 and up. The great thing about this project is there are very few safety concerns, especially if you are using a handheld printer or a spoon for a burnisher. The styrofoam is carved with a ballpoint pen. For this reason, I love this project because it teaches relief printmaking without the concern of carving tools!

A note for printing presses. If you find that students love printmaking and would like to continue exploring this process, I recommend buying a small printmaking press if you have the budget to do so. I got mine several years ago and it is capable of printing small prints, up to about 5x7" in size. I also recently 3D printed a miniature press that actually works quite well! If neither of these are viable options, however, this project works incredibly well with hand burnishers (listed on the materials page) or metal spoons. A bit of pressure is required but the result is still beautiful!

Group Leader Prep

1. Ensure there are enough styrofoam plates cut to size and ready for students to use once they have their sketch.
2. Be prepared to check students' drawings to ensure they are print ready (i.e. no text, or if there is text that it is written backwards, simple design, one color).
3. I prefer to have ink set up and ready to roll before group. To do this, I take a large sheet of plexiglas and set up multiple ink stations (red, blue, yellow, black typically) with rollers next to the ink.
4. When group begins, complete a short demo of spreading ink onto the plexiglas, charging the roller, and rolling ink onto the plate.
5. If using a press, make sure the tension is set correctly for printing the height of the plate you are using.

Group Instructions

1. Think of one activity or subject that you think you are really good at. If you're having trouble thinking of one right now maybe a peer can help.
2. Remember that anything you draw will be printed backward, as all things in printmaking are reversed. I recommend encouraging students to not use text for this reason.

3. Sketch this on a small piece of paper. Drawing our idea before beginning our print is very important.

4. Carefully, begin drawing your design onto your foam with a medium amount of pressure. Or you can trace your design onto your foam with a firm amount of pressure.

5. Using the ink already placed onto a plexiglass, or other smooth surface, roll the brayer onto the ink. It should sound like bacon in a skillet!

6. SLOWLY roll brayer onto foam plate. It should look a little shiny if it is inked well enough to print

7. Place plate onto paper carefully because after the plate has touched the paper, the ink will spread onto the paper. Line up the plate evenly with the paper.

8. Using a handheld printer, or an Intaglio press, with a lot of pressure rub the paper in a circular motion so the ink transfers onto the paper. It is very important you hold the paper still while printing because the paper could slip.

9. Carefully remove paper from plate and you will see your image!

10. Repeat these steps at least one time in order to see the magic of multiples!

Modifications/Autism Considerations

1. I think the biggest consideration for ASD individuals in doing printmaking is making sure there is time to allow for questions and repeating instructions when needed.

2. Having extra staff to support is also a benefit if it is possible - this way, staff can help support students in the details of this project that they may forget.

3. If students have difficulty pressing down into their foam due to fine motor concerns, consider supporting them by tracing their design onto the foam to ensure the liens are deep enough to be printed clearly.

Example

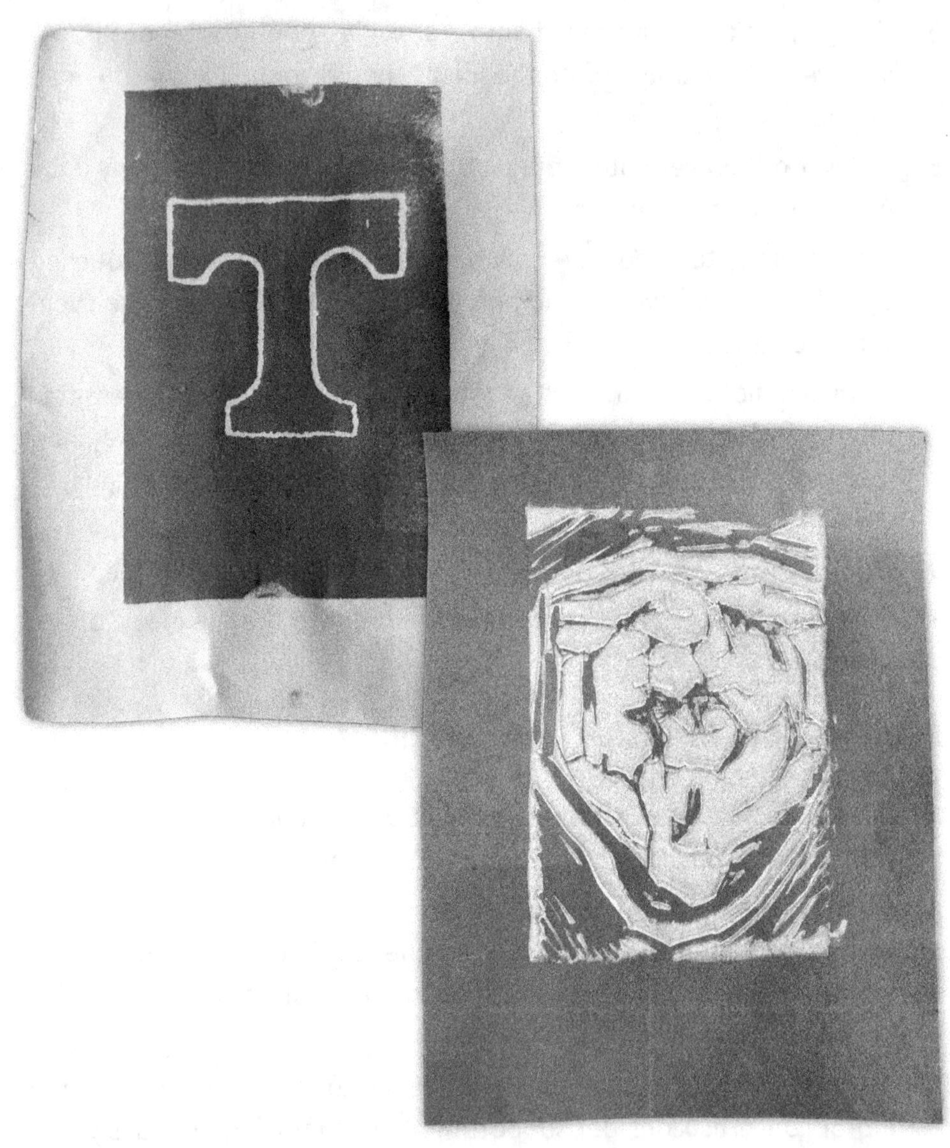

DIRECTIVE 6
Perler Bead Trading Cards

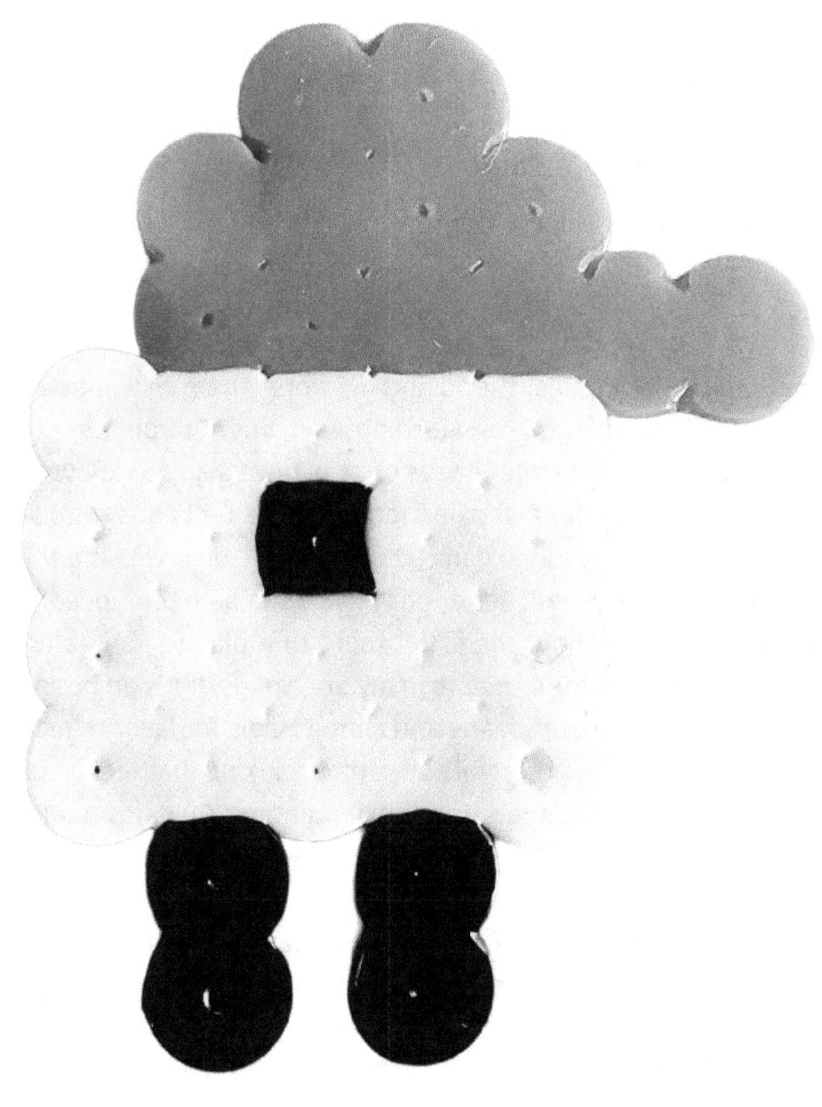

Materials Needed

Perler beads

Perler bead boards

Iron

Parchment paper

Cardstock

Sharpie or black marker

Laminator or packing tape

Perler beads. My greatest friend and my worst enemy. You have not
known true fear until you drop a completed, but not ironed perler bead
creation that a student spent days on. You have also not known true
happiness like a student who just found out perler beads exist and have
created their favorite video game character in 8-bit style. And thus, my
frenemy, the perler bead. Perler beads seem to be either loved or hated
by most who know about them. But these tiny, plastic, meltable beads
are typically a go to for students in my art groups. If it's an open studio,
it is a tie between perler beads and Model Magic for favorite material.
Perler beads offer an accessible view of artmaking that feels more
achievable to students than drawing or painting. There is an outline to
use, as the boards used for perler beads have pegs for each individual
bead to fit onto. The benefit I've noticed for ASD students in my weekly
groups is multifaceted. First, students can easily find patterns for perler
beads online, and many are based on popular characters from games and
movies. Getting to participate in art therapy while also getting to base
it on a preferred interest always excites students, particularly ones with
autism. Secondly, perler beads are meticulous, and many ASD individuals
thrive with repeated actions, such as putting the beads onto each peg.

Thirdly, oftentimes perler beads are surface level, in that what you see is what you get. There are rules to the perler beads and the product, more times than not, is repeatable and consistent.

This trading card project offers students an opportunity to sketch out a character and then watch them come to life through the use of perler beads. This project will take one to two group sessions, depending on size and detail of the perler bead. While this project can be used for any age of students, younger students will likely enjoy the idea of a trading card and characters moreso than older students. This activity will challenge group members to develop a character with not only their physical characteristics, but some personality traits as well. Each student will create a perler bead based on their initial sketch, as well as a small trading card that details traits about their character (template for trading card is included in this book).

Safety considerations for this project really center around the perler bead iron and the harm that could arise if a student were to touch it either accidentally or purposely. I typically carefully collect the unironed perler beads and once the group has left the room, I will iron all of them together. If this is not an option, it is advisable to make sure the iron is away from students and monitored by a staff member.

Group Leader Prep

1. Leader should print out and cut the trading card templates before group begins.
2. Consider having bowls available so that the perler beads can be separated into bowls so multiple students can access various colors at one time.
3. Once group ends, leader will need to iron the perler beads for students, as well as laminate the trading cards, if possible.

Group Instructions

1. Students will sketch out a drawing of a character they would like to create using perler beads.

2. Using perler beads, students will create their character using any colors and shapes they choose. Students can create a small perler bead or a large one, time depending.

3. Once the perler bead is complete, the student will notify the group leader who will set it aside to be ironed once group has concluded.

4. While waiting for their perler bead to be ironed, student will use the trading card template and begin filling in the answers. (See template on the following page)

5. Once the answers are filled in on the trading card, students will decide how they would like their character pictured on their card. Options are as follows:
   - Glue or tape their ironed perler bead onto the card (if size allows)
   - Take a photo and print out picture of the ironed perler bead
   - Draw an image (or use the sketch from the beginning of group) of the character

6. Once finished, student can choose to have their trading card laminated to preserve it.

Modifications/Autism Considerations

1. Allow student to use an existing character if they have difficulty coming up with a novel one.

2. Have perler bead tweezers available for students who may have difficulty with fine motor skills such as pinching.

3. For the trading card, students can choose whether they would like to draw their finished character into the photo slot of the card, tape or glue their perler bead onto the trading card, or take a photo of their perler bead to include on their trading card.

4. I would caution students who like to take their time with details to create a smaller design so that they don't spend weeks finishing their perler bead.

Example

Name: _______________

Age: _______________

Ht/Wt: _______________

Birthplace: _______________

Occupation: _______________

Hobbies: _______________

Special
Talents: _______________

Name: Clive

Age: 147yrs

Ht/Wt: 1'3"

Birthplace: Chicago, IL

Occupation: Pilot

Hobbies: Staying alive

Special
Talents: Balancing my hat on my head

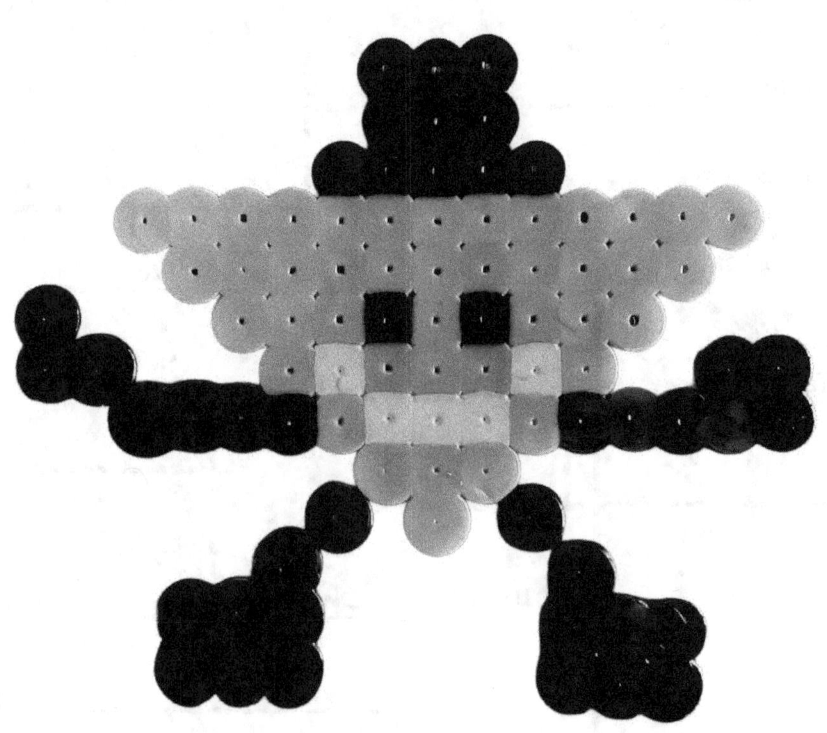

Pastel Watercolor Landscapes

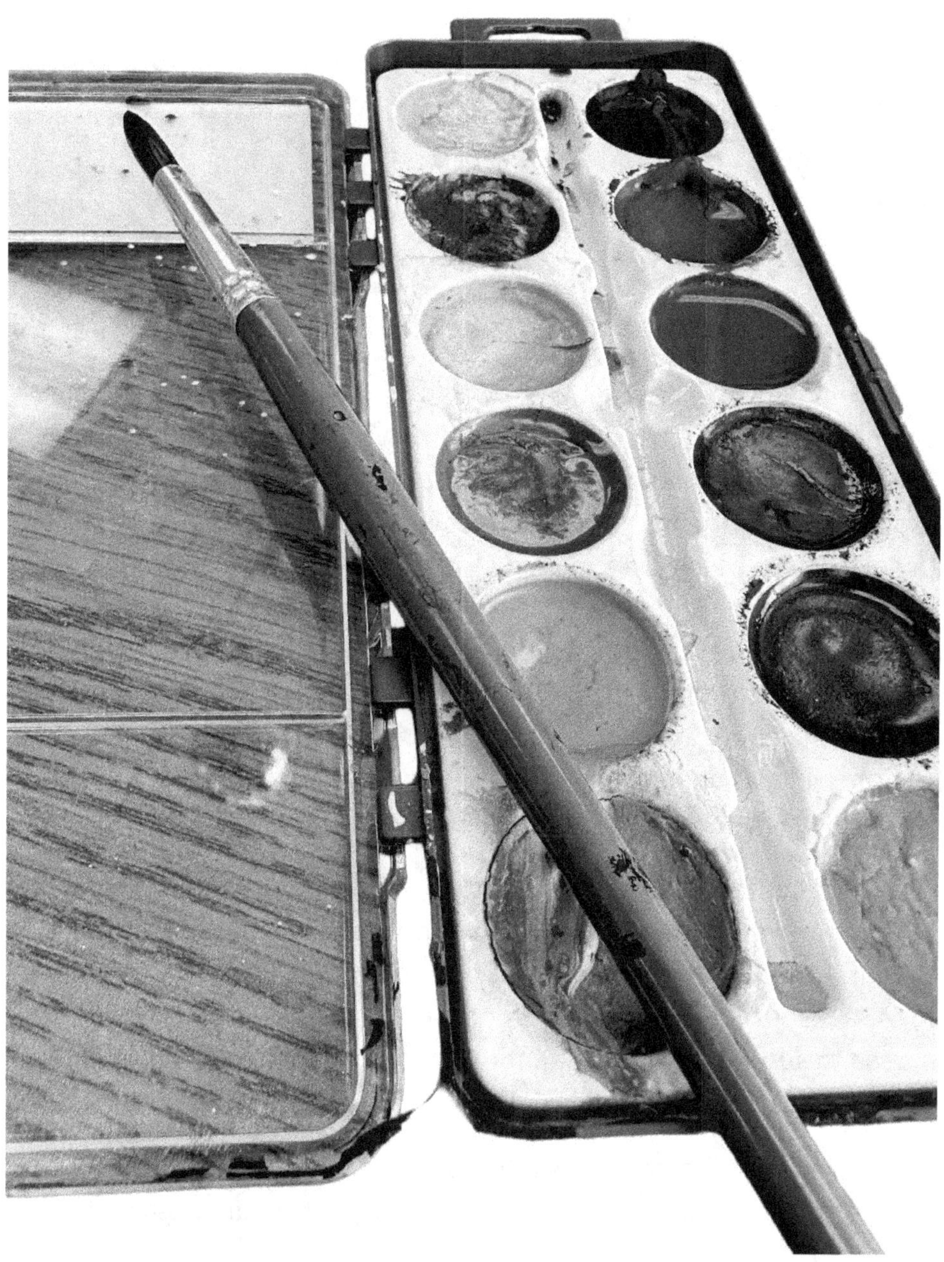

Watercolor! I love it, most of my students do not. However, even within a trauma-informed lens, watercolor can provide a way to not only learn new methods of expressing oneself but also give students a way to explore and experience art in an affective manner. When you add in the oil pastels, which are a more restrictive material (as opposed to the loose material of watercolor), it can allow the activity to become more balanced, and incorporate boundaries that could be missing if oil pastels were not a part of this activity. The oil pastels act as the main material for creating the landscape and then create a resist for the watercolor. It gives students a great opportunity to use a waxier, restrictive tool to draw and then a loose material to wash over the entire landscape.

Not only does this require students to try and explore new materials, but it also gives them a chance to do it in a way that feels manageable. Because the watercolors, which can be a frustrating material particularly for ASD students who prefer contained and structured materials, are only a wash to add a color over the entire drawing, it can be less intimidating than beginning with only watercolors.

A benefit of this directive is also that a landscape can really be anything! It does not have to be a traditional landscape, but could instead be imaginary or inspired by a preferred topic. This can give students more motivation to try this project.

This watercolor/pastel resist activity takes one 40-minute art therapy session and requires little to no preparation for the group leader. This art directive can be used with all school ages of students, though for younger students they may need a watercolor review as well as what landscapes they may be interested in using. I use 9x12" paper, but any size will work great for this directive. Additionally there are no safety concerns for students who may have difficulty keeping themselves safe when sharp objects are involved. Safety concerns could be involved in cases of students with a trauma history using such a loose material as watercolors. As mentioned in "The unique therapeutic effect of different art materials on psychological aspects of 7- to 9-year-old children", the authors note that there has been some research to suggest that each art material falls on a spectrum of rigid to loose and each has unique properties in how clients may relate to them, Pesso-Aviv et al. (2014).

To maintain safety for your group and the students therein, I recommend doing a check-out before the group ends to ensure that students feel safe leaving the group and returning to class. As previously mentioned, the oil pastels add structure in such a way that watercolors become slightly more restrictive than they would be in and of themselves. However, it is always up to the group leader's discretion, based on the students' needs, as to whether this material (or any other) can be used and enjoyed safely.

Group Leader Prep

1. Fill up water cups or bowls for the watercolor portion of the activity.
2. I recommend taping down the corners of the watercolor paper with masking tape so that the paper does not warp.

Group Instructions

1. Create a landscape using one to two oil pastels.
2. The landscape can be imaginary or real.

3. Make sure to press down with some force while drawing so that the pastels leave a waxy texture.

4. The landscape should take up the majority of your paper.

5. Once the landscape is complete, instructor should ensure that the lines are waxy in appearance and feel.

6. Students will get their watercolor palette and a brush to prepare for painting.

7. Once they have their materials, if students have never used watercolors before, I recommend giving a quick demo. This can be individually or for the entire class, depending on skill level.

8. Students should choose a dark color watercolor (i.e. navy blue, purple, or black).

9. For a watercolor wash over the oil pastel resist, the brush should be saturated with water. Each time more paint is put on the brush, more water will be needed.

10. The student will then begin painting over their entire oil pastel landscape.

11. The oil pastel will resist the water and the lines will still be visible even once the watercolor paint is on top of it.

12. Students will continue making sure that the paint has a watery consistency, which allows the watercolor to be loose and have a wash consistency.

13. Once the wash covers the entire paper, the students should leave it taped down to the table until it is dry.

Modifications/Autism Considerations

1. Allow students some freedom in choosing what they will depict in their landscape, including pulling inspiration from preferred topics.
2. If students do not like the oil pastel on their hands, offer gloves.
3. Students can use crayons instead of oil pastels if needed! The same result will occur.
4. Be mindful of students using watercolor if they have difficulty maintaining the cleanliness of their area. I often remind students that their cups of water, if spilled, could damage not only their artwork but their peers' artwork as well.
   - An option would be using watercolor brushes that have a water reservoir within the brush. This cuts down on the need for water cups
   - Another option would be to have a communal cup or bowl so that students do not have water right next to their artwork

Example

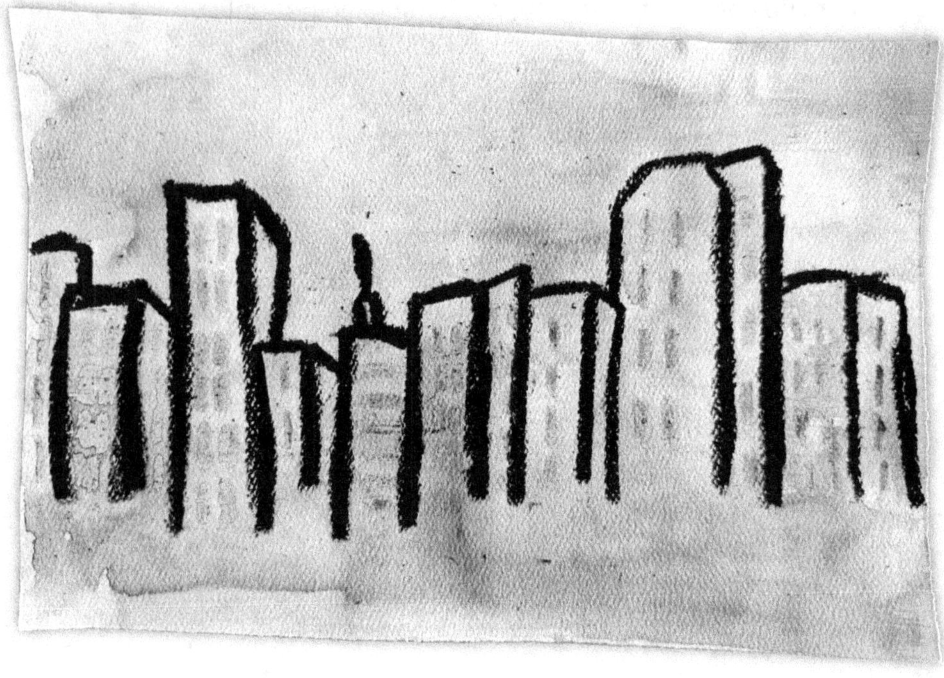

Foil Tape Sculptures

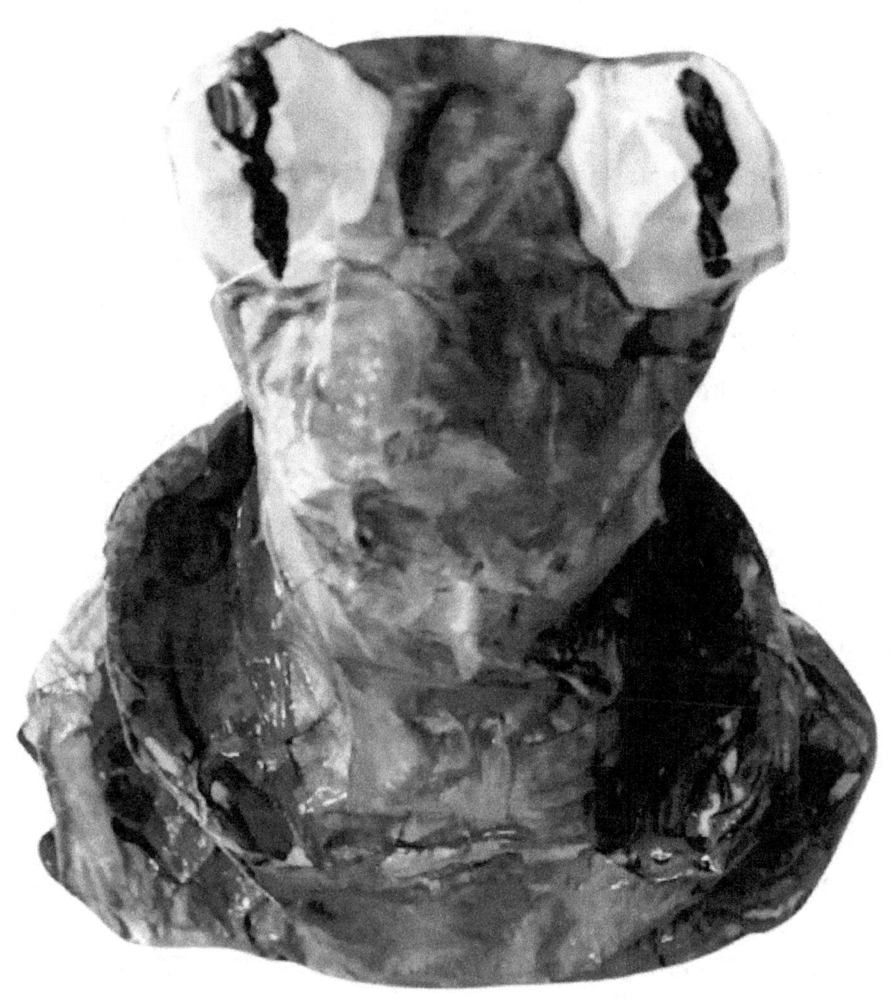

Materials Needed

Aluminum foil

Masking tape

Acrylic paint

Paintbrushes

I love a project that can be done with simple supplies! This one uses aluminum foil and masking tape for the majority of the activity. Further, the acrylic paint does add nice detail, however it can be skipped if needed! This project is fun because on the surface, aluminum foil and tape does not seem like it can be utilized in this way, however students quickly find that as they begin, they are able to create a variety of objects. This directive reminds me of sculptures students can create using wire and plaster, but this one is a much safer alternative as there are no sharp wires or plaster to manage for a group. This directive can be completed in one to two 40-minute group sessions, though I have had groups that needed one extra session to add paint to their creations. One of the benefits of this project is getting to work with students on the challenges that arise when using (at times) uncooperative materials, such as foil. I would recommend this project for middle school and high school students. While students may become frustrated, being able to support them in management of these frustrations while in a contained group allows for safe exploration of these more difficult feelings.

Another benefit to this project is that the theme is wide open for students to choose anything they would like to create with the chosen materials. This allows students to, again, use inspiration from a preferred topic. This will continually motivate students to persevere through the difficulty of materials because they will have a desire to see the completed product.

This art directive is the safe alternative to using something such as wire and plaster, however as with all things, ensuring that students use materials appropriately is a must. For younger students (under 10), be sure they know how to handle the foil, as the edges could potentially cause cuts. This project does not have any group leader prep!

Group Instructions

1. Students will be given a sizable piece of aluminum foil by the art therapy group leader.
2. Students will begin scrunching, folding, etc. the foil in order to begin molding shapes.
    - For animals, consider having students make a large oval, and five small ovals for the body, head and limbs of an animal
    - If students are creating a different sculpture, brainstorm with them as they create to determine what shapes will be most effective for the object they are creating
3. As they create their shapes, they will use masking tape (which should be around the tables) to begin piecing their aluminum foil portions together.
4. It is possible they will need extra hands to complete this part of the activity. Encourage students to pair up to assist one another with this part!
5. All of the foil should be covered in tape, even if more tape is not needed to secure the foil. The entire object should be the color of masking tape. This will make painting easier.
6. Once the sculpture is completely taped together, the students will paint the objects. I allow students to choose as many colors as they need for painting.

Modifications/Autism Considerations

1. Group leader could have the tape strips ready for each place at the table, as well as foil ready for each student already at each seat.
2. Give students parameters for the theme if an open theme is too overwhelming.

3. Likewise, allow only select colors for painting if any number of paints is too much for the student or the space.

4. For ASD students, give extra time as they process the instructions for this project and as they work to piece together their aluminum foil pieces.

Example

Meditative Land Art

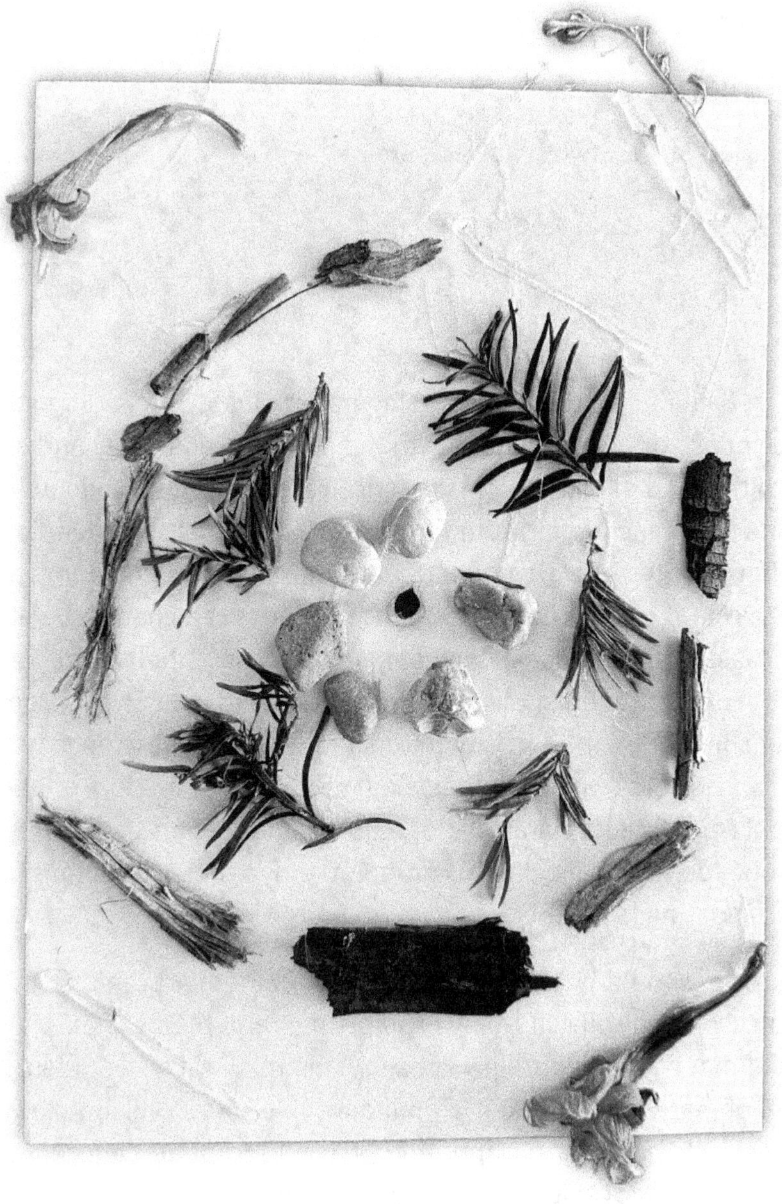

Materials Needed

Canvas

Elmer's glue

Brushes for glue

Hot glue

Assorted leaves, twigs, flowers, etc.

Ziploc bags

Land art is the practice of either using natural materials in order to create a piece of art, or to add materials to the natural land (safely and as not to disturb the land of course). This practice can offer a multitude of benefits, and one of the most important for this population is the grounding it can offer in both collection of materials and in piecing them together into their pattern. This activity also offers students a chance to get out of the classroom or office and go outside to explore their immediate vicinity. For my students, they thrive being able to go on walks, run, and get out some of their energy. With this project, they get to engage in an artmaking process while also enjoying weather and freedom of being outside. For students who may not enjoy traditional art methods, getting to go outside during art therapy group may give them a different outlook on participating in art therapy!

This project should be completed in one 40-minute art therapy group session. I will typically show my example first and then explain what types of plants, rocks, etc we will be looking for. I will give students a history of mandalas and their prominence in eastern religion, however I make sure to go over appropriation (if age appropriate) and why it is important to honor traditions within our own artwork. I have completed this project with middle school and high school students, as younger than middle school has some difficulty staying on task when outside. The ASD students I have worked with love getting to procure what items they need in order to create a meditative art piece.

There are a few safety concerns to be aware of when planning and implementing this activity. One, make sure that students you are taking outside can keep themselves safe while outside. For my students, there are times when individuals may not be able to go outside due to safety concerns. In that case, we would not complete this activity or would make modifications as needed. Additionally, ensure that if you are working in a school, you have the appropriate number of staff with the group as you go on a nature walk. For our organization, we want to have at least two staff, but three would be preferred for an activity such as this. I also like to have a conversation with students about what type of nature materials we should leave untouched and which ones are appropriate to take. I encourage students to use only plants that have already fallen off of the branch or stem so as not to damage growing plants. Lastly, If a hot glue gun is needed to adhere bigger or heavier items to the canvas, make sure staff can monitor usage of it or can implement usage of it for the students.

Group Leader Prep

1. Prepare gallon size ziploc bags for each student in the group. Write their names on each bag.
2. Ensure each student has a canvas as well. I prefer to put names on the canvases as well, so that as students begin putting their items onto the canvas, they don't have to worry about that small detail.
3. This may go without saying, but make sure to check the weather before implementing this project. Rain or hail or snow would not be ideal for this activity. Have a backup directive ready in case the weather does not cooperate!
4. Prepare small cups of Elmer's white glue for students to use once they need to glue down their materials. I also have students use old brushes or inexpensive brushes to use for the glue.

Group Instructions

1. After giving a pre-teach about outside expectations, as well as what students will be looking for, students should line up to go outside and begin the nature walk.

    - Remind students that this walk should be calming and provide a grounding experience for students.
    - If students seem like they need an exercise before beginning the nature walk, consider completing a meditative activity, such as a breathing routine or the 1-2-3-4-5 grounding technique (one thing you can see, one thing you can touch, one thing you can smell, one thing you can hear, one thing you can taste).

2. Once students are outside, they will walk as a group and begin locating materials they find interesting. I caution that if it is any bigger than their palm, it will be too large for their art piece.

    - Another quick note for safety is that I will allow students to find small rocks or pebbles to use but make sure students are not trying to bring in anything that could pose a risk of danger to students.

3. As students find natural items outside, they will collect them in their Ziploc bags. I require students to have at least eight to ten items in their bags before returning inside.

4. Once all students have their materials, they will return inside to begin their design of their final land art mandala.

5. I recommend students lay out their items in the design they desire before gluing anything down to the canvas.

    - As noticed in the image at the beginning of this directive, the pattern is circular. However, in the examples, the pattern is more abstracted. Students can choose however they would like to plan out their directive. But I do require the planning portion of the project.

6. Once students have used most (or all) of their natural materials, then they will use their glue brush and cup of Elmer's glue to begin

adhering their objects to the canvas. They should put glue onto the canvas and then place the object onto the glue. It becomes too messy to put glue on the item.

7. They will continue this process until each of their planned items is fully adhered to the canvas.

8. At this time, if students have a few items that need to be hot glued down, I will have a station set up for them to either use the hot glue gun (if age appropriate) or to bring their canvas to staff in order to have help putting their item onto the canvas.

9. Once finished, they will set their canvas onto a drying rack or drying area so that it can dry.

10. Before students leave the art room, I make sure to have them wipe down their area in case any glue gets on the table.

Modifications/Autism Considerations

1. If your group is large or if students need more support, consider taking the students in small groups on the nature portion of the walk. If this takes more time than allotted in the description, this project could be split into two sessions.

2. If students are unable to choose items on a walk, but you would still like them to be outside, the group instructor could pre-choose an abundance of items and have them in a designated area outside (such as a courtyard or front yard of a building).

3. If there is space and students have the capacity to do so, consider having the entire group outdoors instead of returning inside to design and glue the items to the canvas.

    - This would require extra planning for group leader as all glue and canvases would need to be prepared and placed outside before the group begins.

4. Lastly, I have attached a circular template for your use on the following page if students are having a tough time understanding how to arrange their natural materials. This could be given just as a visual or students could glue down the template onto their canvas or trace it onto the canvas before beginning gluing.

Template

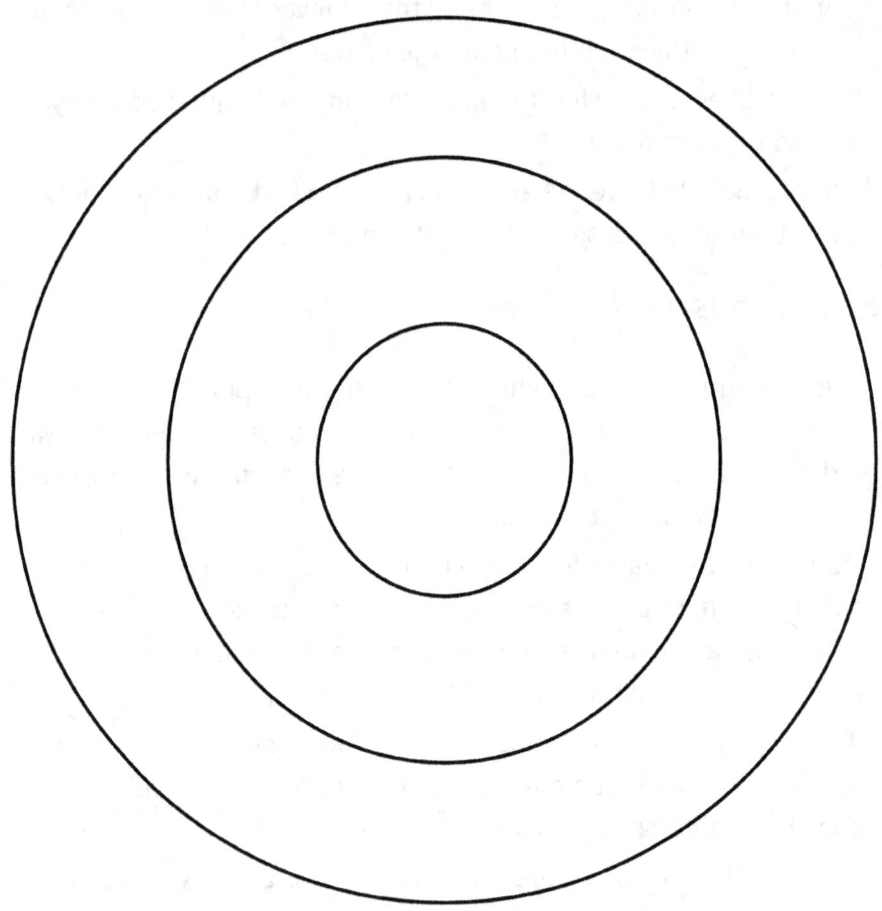

Example

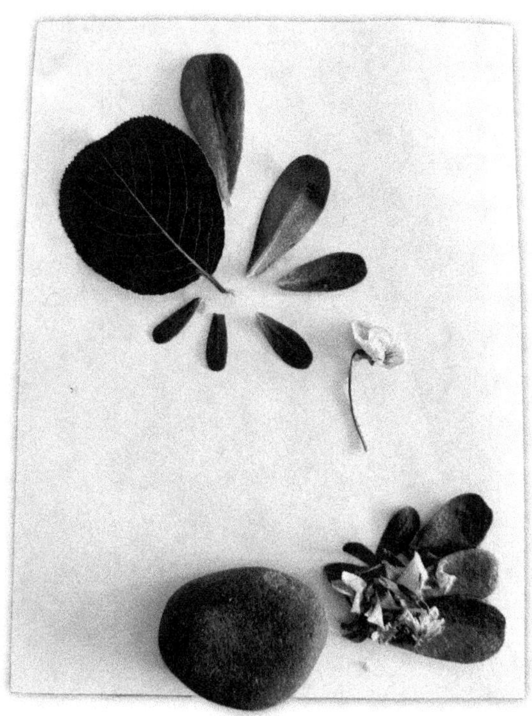

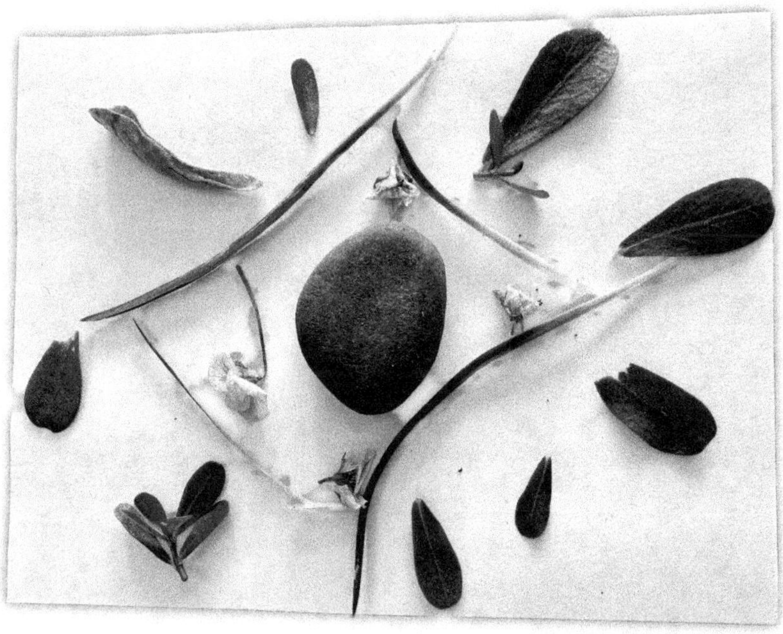

Reverse Coloring with Alternative Mark Making

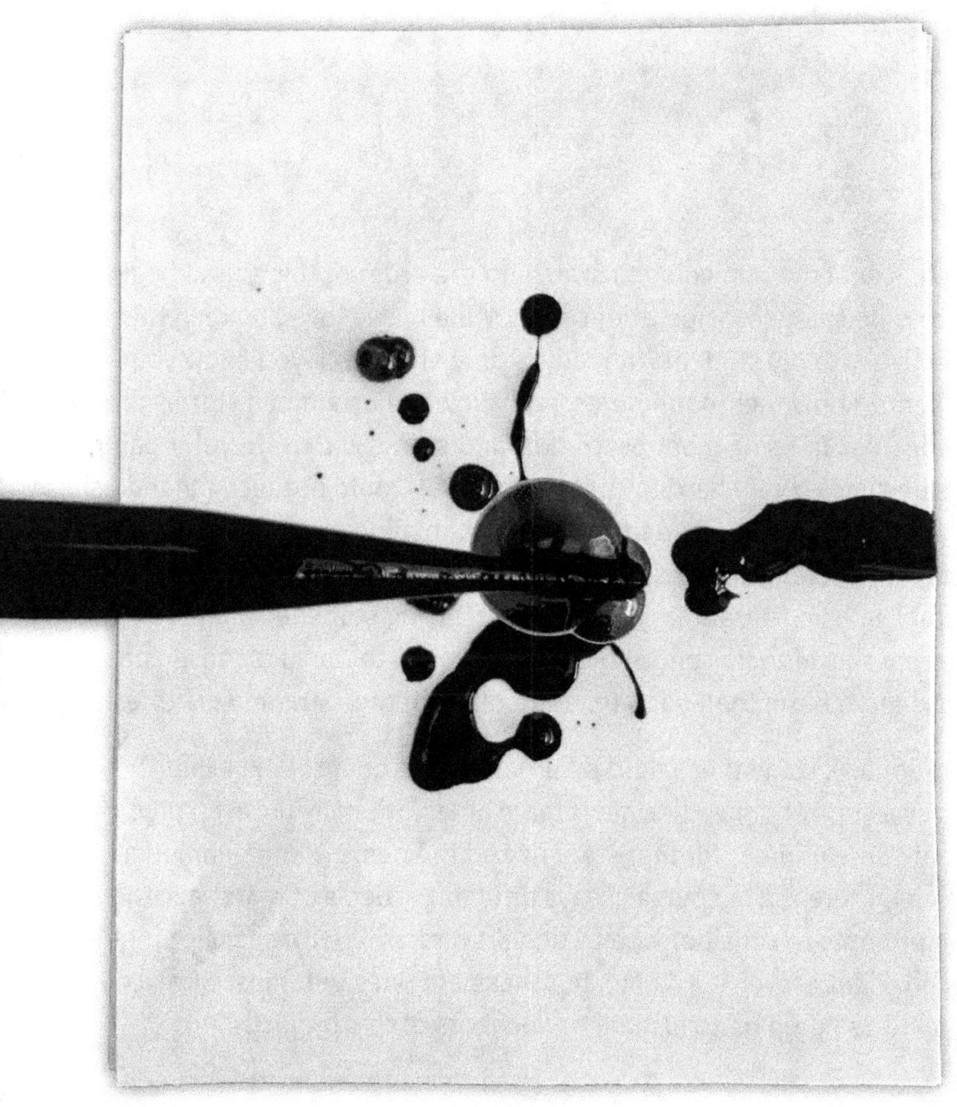

Materials Needed

Watercolor paper

Pipettes, Q-Tips, straws,
foam brushes, combs

Liquid Watercolor

Sharpies, or other black markers

Salt

Dish soap

For this directive, I'm going to switch up the order of things and begin with some safety considerations first! While I have loved leading this directive with my students, it really is only effective if you know your students, know their boundaries, and know their trauma histories (if applicable). In using pipettes, combs, and straws with watercolor paint, this becomes a very hard to control project. I would not recommend using this activity with ASD students younger than middle school and I would not recommend using this with students who have a significant trauma history. In using a trauma-informed lens, giving students a material that they have little to no control over can induce a trauma response and cause more harm than good for students with these trauma histories.

Additionally, using these fluid materials with students who exhibit impulse control difficulties may create an emotionally (or even physically) unsafe environment for that student and the peers in their immediate vicinity. There are of course always different aspects of materials, themes, and prompts to consider when using art directives with specific students (as no client is ever the same), but these are ones that most often come to mind as I prepare to explain the benefits of this project!

This directive is a two-week project and as mentioned previously, should be completed with students in middle or high school. It does require some preparation for the group leader, however provides a fun and exciting opportunity for students to experiment with materials and processes they may not otherwise be able to use.

Students will get to use any materials set up on the table and play around with what patterns, designs, shapes, etc they can create only using these alternative methods and not the traditional watercolor palette and brush (as seen in Directive 7). This project allows ASD students to have freedom in what they create through the use of alternative methods and reintroduces structure in the second portion of the project as they find shapes, patterns, and lines while implementing the 'reverse coloring book' method.

For the alternative mark making portion of the directive, they will have the chance to use pipettes (as seen in the image on page 69), toothbrushes, and stiffened paintbrushes to splatter, drop, spread, etc watercolor paint onto their watercolor paper. Additionally, students can use dish soap and watercolor paint in a cup and with a straw, blow bubbles onto their paper. This creates beautiful and nuanced circular forms onto their paper. Lastly, students can then use combs, toothpicks, foam brushes, etc to move the paint around on their paper. While this can create a situation in the art room that can be harder to contain, I have found that with a pre-teach and specific expectations given prior to beginning, students actually have done very well with learning these new methods for mark making.

Once the paint has dried (typically the following session), students will use Sharpies to begin creating formed borders and highlight already seen patterns within their watercolor marks. The reverse coloring method has gained popularity in recent years, and many people have published books to highlight this trend! Giving students a chance to be a part of an up and coming art therapeutic trend can be a cool experience for them, and one that can even boost their self confidence and esteem. This project is beneficial for ASD students not only because of the freedom it provides, but also because in the first portion of this project, there are so few rules to artmaking that they can again, increase their self efficacy over their artwork that may not otherwise be possible. Lastly, a benefit is it is just really fun to engage with your students in a way that is unique and that offers so many "happy accidents" as they work!

Group Leader Prep

1. Set up multiple bowls and/or cups with various liquid watercolors. I typically have the students choose between three and four colors. Any more than this can create a muddied effect on their finished artwork.

2. Spread out a tarp or newspaper over the tables/desks the students will be using for the experimentation portion of the project.

3. If you have plastic trays, set up a piece of watercolor paper on a tray for each student. I use plastic lunch trays for this and other projects. This will help contain the materials a bit more than only using the wide open table.

4. WRITE NAMES ON THE BACK OF THE WATERCOLOR PAPER. I did not do this the first time I led this group project, and it did not go well.

5. Place pipettes, straws, toothbrushes, stiffened paint brushes, and any other materials students will have access to for this directive, onto the center of the table.

6. Pre-teach students and give clear expectations, for ASD specifically, as to what rules there are for these materials, as well as what they will be expected to complete.

7. Prepare dish soap (1 tsp), water, and four drops of watercolor paint into small cups for bubble blowing. Make sure students all have their own straws so that students do not inadvertently share a straw.

8. For the second half of the project, group leader should just make sure each student's watercolor design dries and is ready for mark making on top of the paper.

Group Instructions

1. Students will sit at the table in front of their watercolor paper (with their name on it).
2. Group leader will demonstrate how to use the various materials.
3. After students watch the demo, they will begin with one alternative mark making method.
4. Students can repeat one method or try up to three methods (with up to three different colors).
5. If students have time and wish to do more than one, they may complete a second one.
6. Once the watercolor paintings are complete and dry (following session), students will use a Sharpie and begin the "reverse coloring" method and begin drawing back in lines to create structure and form on top of the mark making.
7. Students should take no less than 30 minutes to complete this portion.

Modifications/Autism Considerations

1. Consider having fewer options for materials, if having all of them set out on the table will feel overwhelming to your specific group of students.
2. If Sharpies are not available, any type of black marker will work.
3. When students are outlining in the second part of this activity, they may need examples given as to what they are looking for if they have never participated in an exercise such as this.
4. For students that may have difficulty with impulse control or the ability to keep their materials to just their paper, consider having students sit further apart from one another, and consider covering the entire table with plastic tarp.

Example

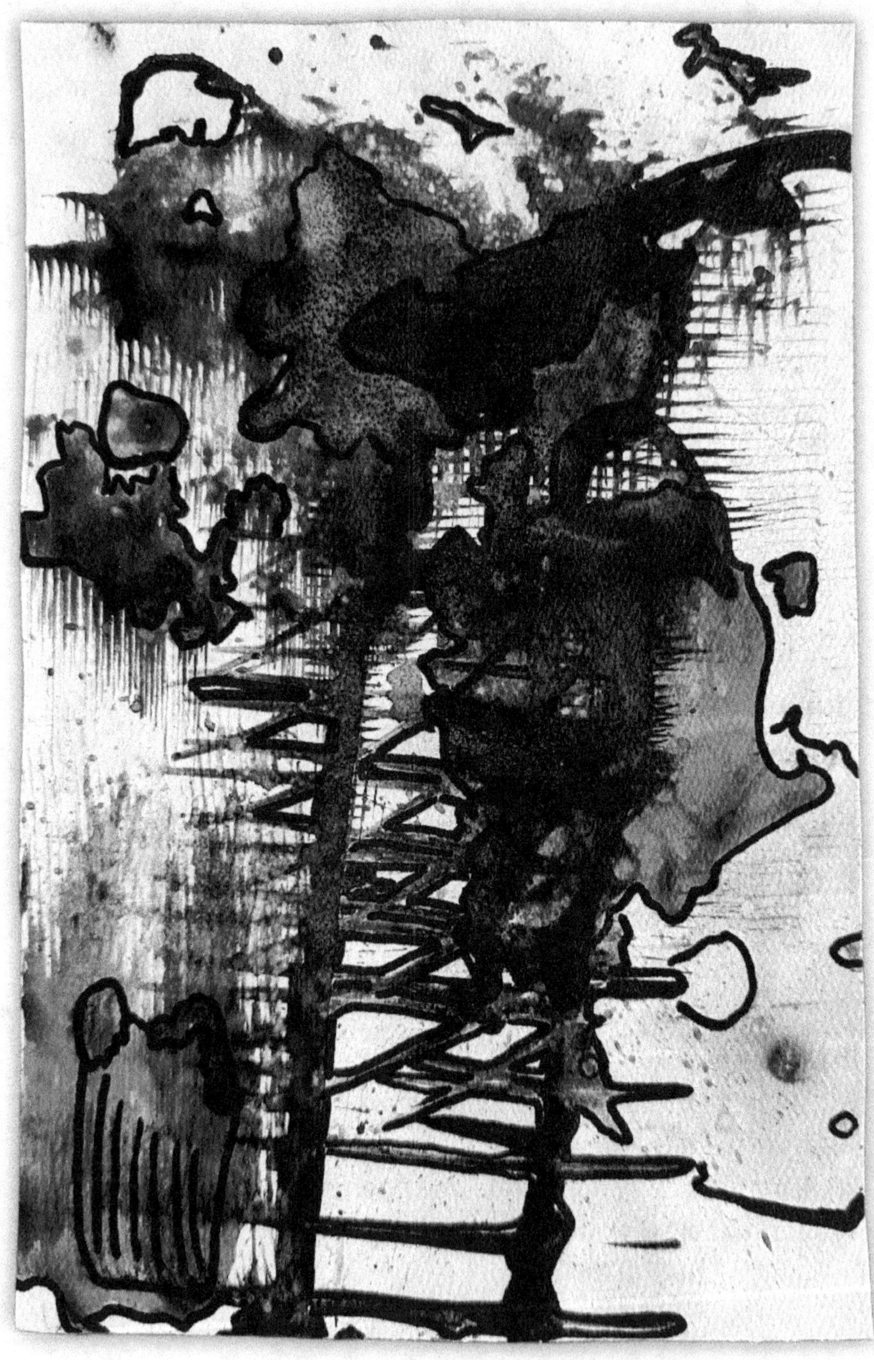

DIRECTIVE 11

Safe Space Box

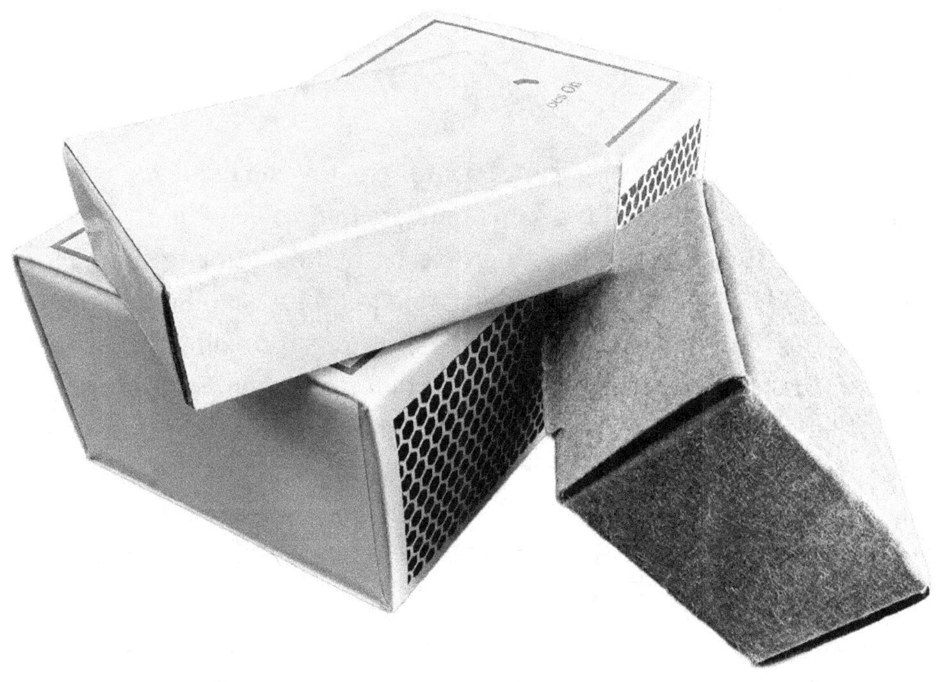

Materials Needed

Model Magic

Sequins, or other decorative additions

Paint or makers, if desired

Miniature boxes

    Matchboxes

    Origami boxes

    Miniature cardboard boxes

Similar to my love for books, is my love for creating small microcosms with my students. Some of the same benefits that come with bookmaking, such as honoring experiences, creating intimate spaces for the artist and viewer to see, and being able to freeze a moment in time, are also found in small sculptural boxes. This miniature directive allows students to choose items or experiences that make them feel safe and encapsulate them into a relic of their own creation. This project also gives students an opportunity to hone their fine motor skills, as they have to create small items to fit inside their box. I love doing this project with students because what is important to them may not be important to me and vice versa. By giving them choice and control over what goes inside their box, they not only get to have the final say but also they become motivated to complete this project as they work with their preferred subjects.

Because this project can be completed with a variety of spaces, such as matchboxes, origami boxes, bakery boxes, miniature cardboard boxes, there are limitless possibilities for group leaders and students, even if budgets are slim. Additionally, students can choose to leave their box the color it is or add a little pizazz or color to it, as it fits with their desires and personalities. This project is also a great multimedia project for students to get experience with as it uses both the box, as well as Model Magic for the items found inside the box. Students have an opportunity to express themselves in multiple modalities, while also curating a space that allows them to find safety, happiness, and even perhaps one of their coping skills.

This directive is best completed in two sessions, however can be done in one if needed, as it suits the students. I have completed this project with all school ages, from 8-21, and have found success with each level. Another added benefit of this directive is that there are few, if any safety concerns. The materials used are restrictive, and students do not need access to any sharps in completing this directive. Additionally, Model Magic offers students the ability to explore safely because Model Magic is forgiving when mistakes are made!

Group Leader Prep

1. The boxes I use for this activity are almost like a cardstock and must be folded before use. There are lines for folding instructions, but consider folding them or scoring them before group so that the students can focus on creating the items inside the boxes.
2. If paint or other accouterments will be used, collect them and have them ready for your group.

Group Instructions

1. Students will choose a box to be their container for their project. If there are various sizes or types, allow students to choose which one they would like to use.
2. The students will then choose if they would like to decorate the outside (or inside) of their box using paint, sequins, or other arts and crafts. If they choose to do this, encourage students to decorate the box based on aspects of their personality.

3. Once their boxes are complete, students will use Model Magic to begin constructing at least two to three miniature items to fit inside their safe box.
    - Students should focus on what things, or representation of things, make them feel safe or at ease
    - Keep in mind that traditional things that may make us feel safe may look different for our ASD students
4. Students will mold their items. Group leader can be available for support as needed.
5. Once students have created their objects, they will have two options.
6. If students wish to color or paint their objects, they will wait until the Model Magic dries, and then color it. Once this has been completed, they will place them in their box.
7. If the student used colored Model Magic, or they wish to keep their Model Magic white, they will place them into their box.
8. If some students are finished the following week, and others are still working, consider implementing an open studio session so that all students can finish their project without other students moving further ahead on a different directive.

Modifications/Autism Considerations

1. If ASD students have difficulty while working with miniature items, consider using a large box such as a bakery box or a mailing box so that they become comfortable working in this way.
2. As mentioned previously, encourage students to really think about what they want in their box. However, if a student chooses a video game console or a preferred card game, for instance, do not discourage this. Often students see value in very different ways than we do and these items may offer a lot of comfort and support to them!
3. If students have trouble coming up with items to put in their box, they could brainstorm ideas on a scratch sheet of paper before they begin molding with the Model Magic.
4. If you have a student that is willing to participate but has difficulty molding or coming up with ideas, you could choose to allow them to google an image or use collage items in place of Model Magic.

Example

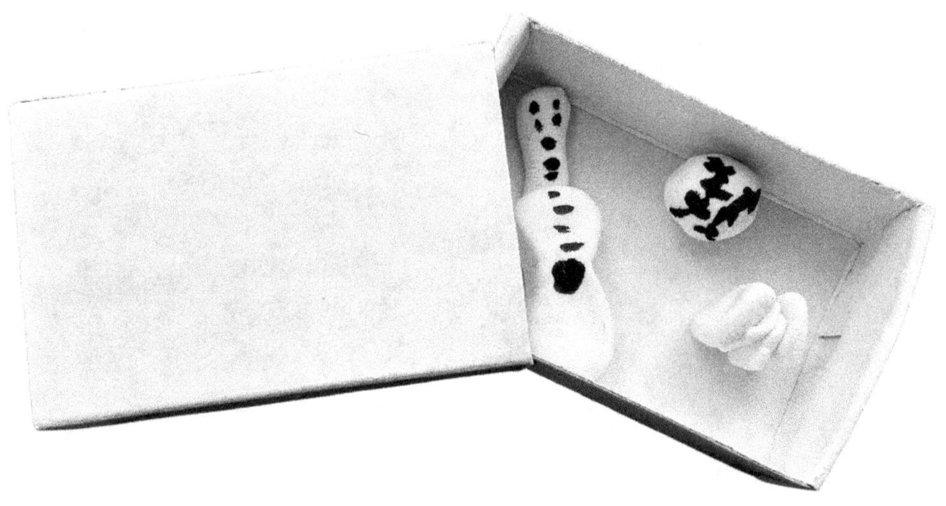

Torn Paper Self-Portraits

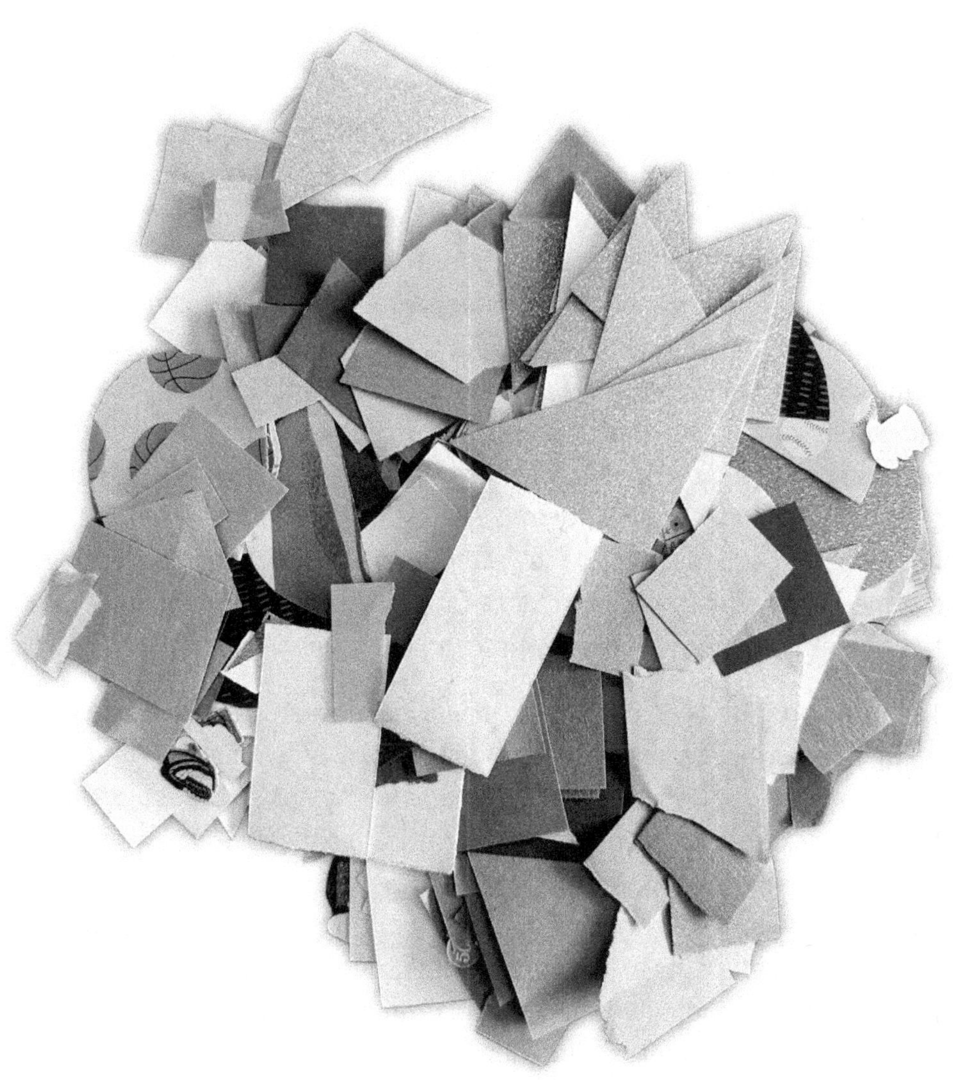

Torn paper self-portraits! The answer to all of those scraps from collage days and the leftover ends to cut down paper! Beyond the obvious benefit of disallowing art materials to go to waste, this project also gives students an opportunity to create a self-portrait using existing materials, rather than drawing or painting. Jumping into self-portraits can be triggering for some students, especially if ASD students may not have a full sense of self or identity yet. During these formative years, social difficulties crop up for students and asking them to draw a realistic self-portrait may be quite difficult for these clients. Because of these factors, giving students an opportunity to create either how they see themselves, how others see them, or how they want others to see them. This can put a sometimes needed barrier in place for protection as students navigate their identity through art exploration and expression.

The torn paper bits can come from magazine pieces, scraps, or can be cut up by a group leader before the group begins. It is recommended to make sure there are a variety of shades of the paper scraps so that students from all backgrounds have pieces that they can choose from. This project only takes one session, and can be a great "get to know you" activity for students new to group or at the beginning of the year. I have done this directive with students as young as middle school and as old as upper high school. Depending on the age, the prompt can change slightly to reflect the development of students in the group. For instance, younger students may only be able to manage a self-portrait of how you see yourselves. As they get older, you can deepen the prompt and perhaps have them do two portraits side by side: How you see yourselves, how others see you.

I love doing this project with ASD students because they see things so differently than I do and I love watching their creativity come to life with these existing materials. Additionally, another benefit is because it is tearing paper and then gluing to the drawing paper with a glue stick, there are no physical safety concerns for students of all ages. I would caution that any student that may be having significant difficulties with self-image may need extra support to create either an abstracted version of their self-portrait or modify the prompt slightly and have them create a collage that highlights parts of their identity.

Group Leader Prep

1. If using scrap magazine pieces or full magazines, ensure they are appropriate for school use.
2. Once you have the paper, set out drawing paper for students, as well as glue sticks.
3. Separate the scrap papers and/or magazines around the table so that students will have a variety to choose from that is in arm's reach.

Group Instructions

1. Students will choose either scrap paper or magazine pages that they find interesting.
2. Pre-teach students that they can either create an accurate face or they can make an abstracted self-portrait as well, in which they can choose their favorite colors or things and arrange them to build their portrait.
3. Once they have their pieces, they will tear them to size and begin forming their self-portrait.
4. Students will arrange their pieces onto their drawing paper and begin gluing each one down with their glue stick.
5. As they work, they can continue tearing paper to add details or to add more colors to their portraits.

6. Once completed, they will put their names on the back of their drawings and if there is time, share with the group as they are comfortable.

7. If doing this project at the beginning of the group, it is a great time to share something important that was added to the collage so that peers and staff can begin to get to know them better!

Modifications/Autism Considerations

1. If students have difficulty understanding how to collage a self-portrait, consider printing out a basic face template and have them fill in the spaces with their paper scraps.

2. If students have trouble tearing due to perfectionism in art, you can allow them to use scissors as long as appropriate safety measures are taken.

3. At times individuals may become distracted with magazine pages, and if this is the case then consider having all scraps torn or cut down before group so that students do not spend their time looking through magazines.

4. Depending on the level of ASD students and their fine motor skills, they may have difficulty tearing small pieces and then gluing them. If this occurs, they can spread glue onto the paper and then put pieces on top of the glue, rather than gluing each individual piece.

5. As mentioned previously, depending on the student they may have more difficulty with their self-image than others. If this occurs, give students alternative ideas, such as a collage highlighting their likes and/or dislikes, favorite color, etc.

6. Lastly, especially for students that may have a tough time with executive functioning, leave time to clean up the space! Those tiny paper pieces have a knack for finding their way to the floor and in chairs. Encourage students to work with their peers to clean up the art space before heading back to class!

Example

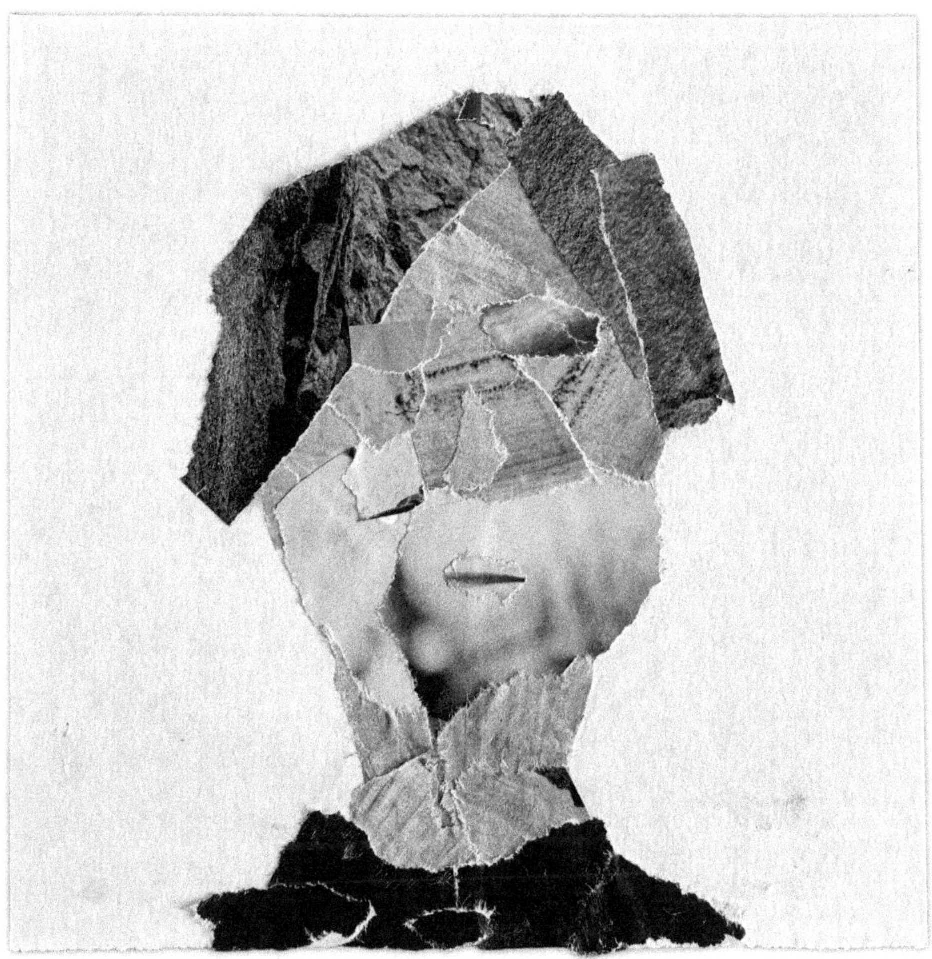

DIRECTIVE 13

All About Me Collages

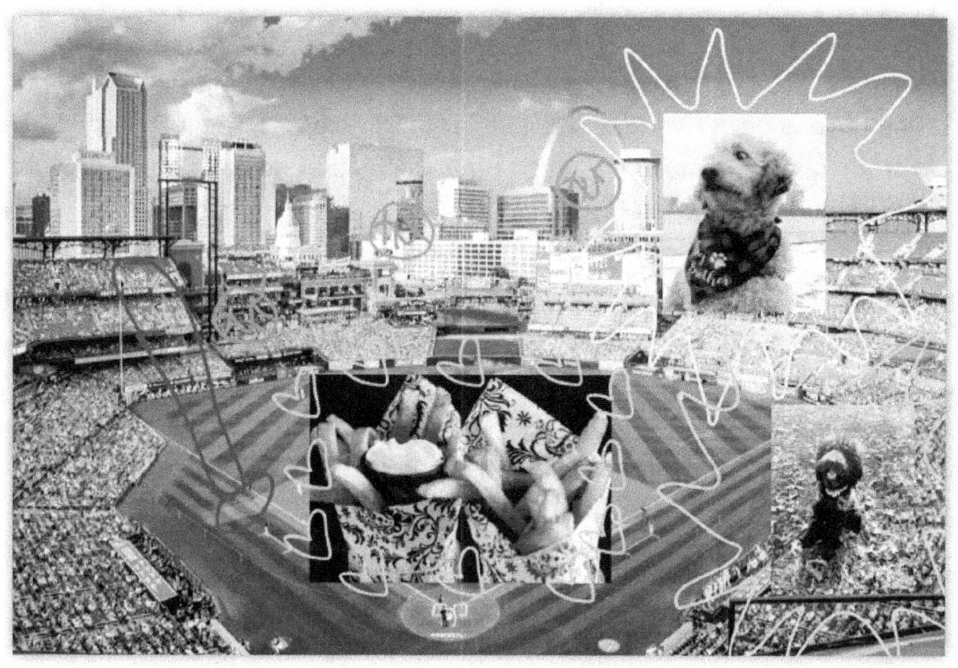

Materials Needed

Magazine or newspaper
clippings

Scissors

Markers

Glue sticks

Drawing paper

I like to consider this project as a sister to Directive 12, the torn paper
self-portraits. And at times, I even offer them as a choice to students
in the same art group. I love collages. LOVE them! It is a project that
allows students to practice executive functioning and planning, both of
which can be difficult for students on the spectrum. This collage gives
students an opportunity to create a collage that is, as the title states,
all about them. Collages are, as noted earlier in this book, part of Hinz's
theory in "The Expressive Therapies Continuum" (2009). They fall on the
cognitive and symbolic level, and give students maybe one of their first
opportunities to practice finding symbols that represent aspects of their
identity. This level can be difficult for younger students, however giving
them images already in existence (i.e. magazine clippings), supports them
in the exploration of learning about symbolism.

For ASD students, they may find symbolism in different places than
neurotypical students might, and they are often drawn to images that
appear in preferred topics (i.e. games, anime, etc.). Because of this, I
caution you to have a plethora of different magazines on hand that cover
some of these popular topics. It goes easier for the group leader - trust
me. This project can really be completed with all ages inside a school.
For my younger students, I have them choose three to five images that

they like while flipping through magazine clippings. Because they are in elementary and middle school, they might not yet be able to form deep meaning between images and their identity. However, they can participate in building a collage that tells a bit about them and what is important to them that they can share with their peers.

As mentioned, this activity can be completed with modifications for any age. It can also be directed in one 40-minute group therapy session. I make sure when prepping for this activity that magazines are school appropriate and already torn out of the magazine. This is to help students not become distracted with the entirety of the magazine, which can cause students to lose focus on the project at hand. For younger students, as mentioned I have them choose three to five images that show aspects of what they like or dislike. For older students, I encourage them to pick images that represent them. Older students are directed to choose at least five images. When I lead this group directive, I engage students in a conversation about symbolism in art and how that can apply to them. It is really powerful to see students choose images that they connect with because as we know, art therapy provides meaning and expression when words cannot. With something as a collage, it can open the door for students to begin even deeper explorations through images.

When considering group safety, it is important to highlight that scissors are used for this activity. If students are not able to keep themselves safe and use scissors appropriately, I recommend having students tear images out, similar to the torn paper self-portrait. If students are able to safely use scissors, I hand out the scissors to each student and each pair is correlated with a number so that I ensure each pair comes back to me before the end of group.

Group Leader Prep

1. Ensure all magazines are appropriate. For my students, this means no weapons, no sexualized images, and no curse words. If you're not in a school this could differ, but for our art therapy groups we follow school rules as closely as we can.
2. If you have magazines that have not been read through, read through

them and then cut out clippings. I have a collage station so that I can have all of my magazine cutouts separated into genres. This of course isn't necessary, but I have found it helps students determine what they want to begin looking for. This can lessen the pressure of the prompt if students have never done an activity such as this previously.

3. Make sure scissors are numbered and glue sticks are fresh!

4. Any size paper will work for this activity and I recommend drawing paper. I typically have students use either 9x12 or even 5x7 for younger students. Make sure this paper is available and cut down to size before group begins.

Group Instructions

1. Engage students in a discussion, if appropriate, about symbolism and how they may find images that portray aspects of their identity (i.e. video game that they enjoy, favorite food, an image of a family that reminds them of their family, a home, etc.).

2. Remind students that they will need either three to five or at least five, depending on the age group of which you are leading.

3. Students will then begin looking through folders or groupings of magazine clippings based on what type of imagery they are seeking.

4. If safe to do so, at this time the group leader should pass out scissors to students. IF scissors are not available for this group, instruct students to carefully tear out what images they are drawn to in the magazine clippings.

5. Students should gather their images first before beginning the gluing portion of this activity.

6. Students will collect their images into a pile near their place at the table or desk.

7. Once they have their images, direct each individual to lay out their composition onto their paper before they glue.

8. After they have laid it out as they would like it, they may begin gluing down their images. Make sure they glue down all of the edges and corners of each picture so that they do not curl up while drying.

9. Once they are finished, they will flip the collage to the back and they will write their name, as well as what each of the images represents to them.

10. Once completed, they will return scissors and glue and will then clean their area of leftover scraps or glue. Remind them to check the floor around them as well!

11. If there is time, and if students are willing, allow each group member to share all of their collage or a part of their collage with the group. This is a great time for students and group leaders to understand more of each individual.

Modifications/Autism Considerations

1. For this activity, there is a sizable modification that I often make for my ASD group participants. This modification is allowing students to use Google Draw or another online program to create their collage. I do this for a few reasons, and they are as follows:

   - Some students are going to have difficulty finding the exact images they resonate with while looking through magazines. If they are using a school issued computer, they can use Google Images to curate their about me collage.

   - Students may really have a sensory issue with glue and even the feeling of magazine clippings. If they are using their computer, there is very little sensory component involved.

   - Typically ASD students are savvy with technology and they may have more buy-in to attempting this directive if they get to use their computer for an art project.

   - If you are conducting virtual group or individual sessions, this is a fantastic way to get students making art if they do not have art materials at their fingertips.

   The downside to this is of course that ideally we get our students off of technology and into using physical materials as they explore and express their identity through artmaking. However, if a student is willing to participate and try with the assistance of tech, then I want them to feel excited and proud of their work!

2. Another modification that can be made for this activity is keeping the glue off of the tables until all magazines have been rifled through and chosen. This allows students a chance to work in sequential order, thus increasing executive functioning skills, and it also keeps glue from getting on unused magazine clippings.

3. If students are having difficulty coming up with images that represent them, give them an opportunity to look for their favorite food or favorite animal, among other prompts. Breaking it down for them into small pieces may help them begin to understand further what it means to have symbols based on their life and/or identity.

Example

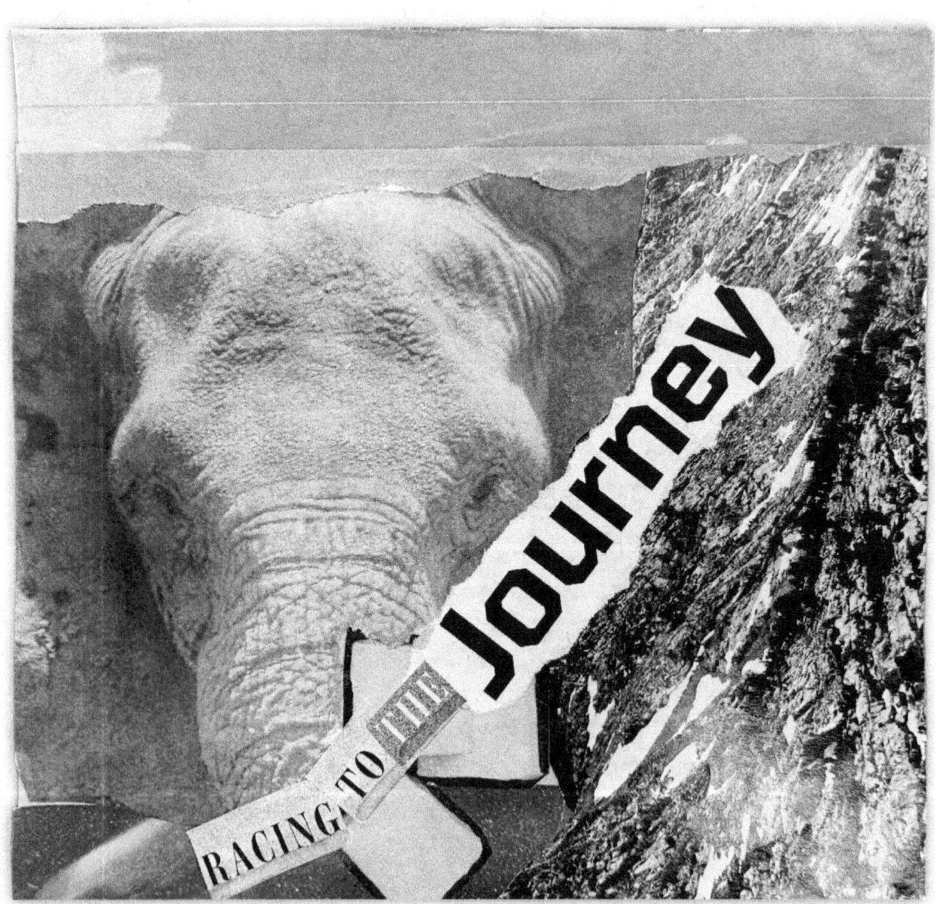

Sewn Pillows

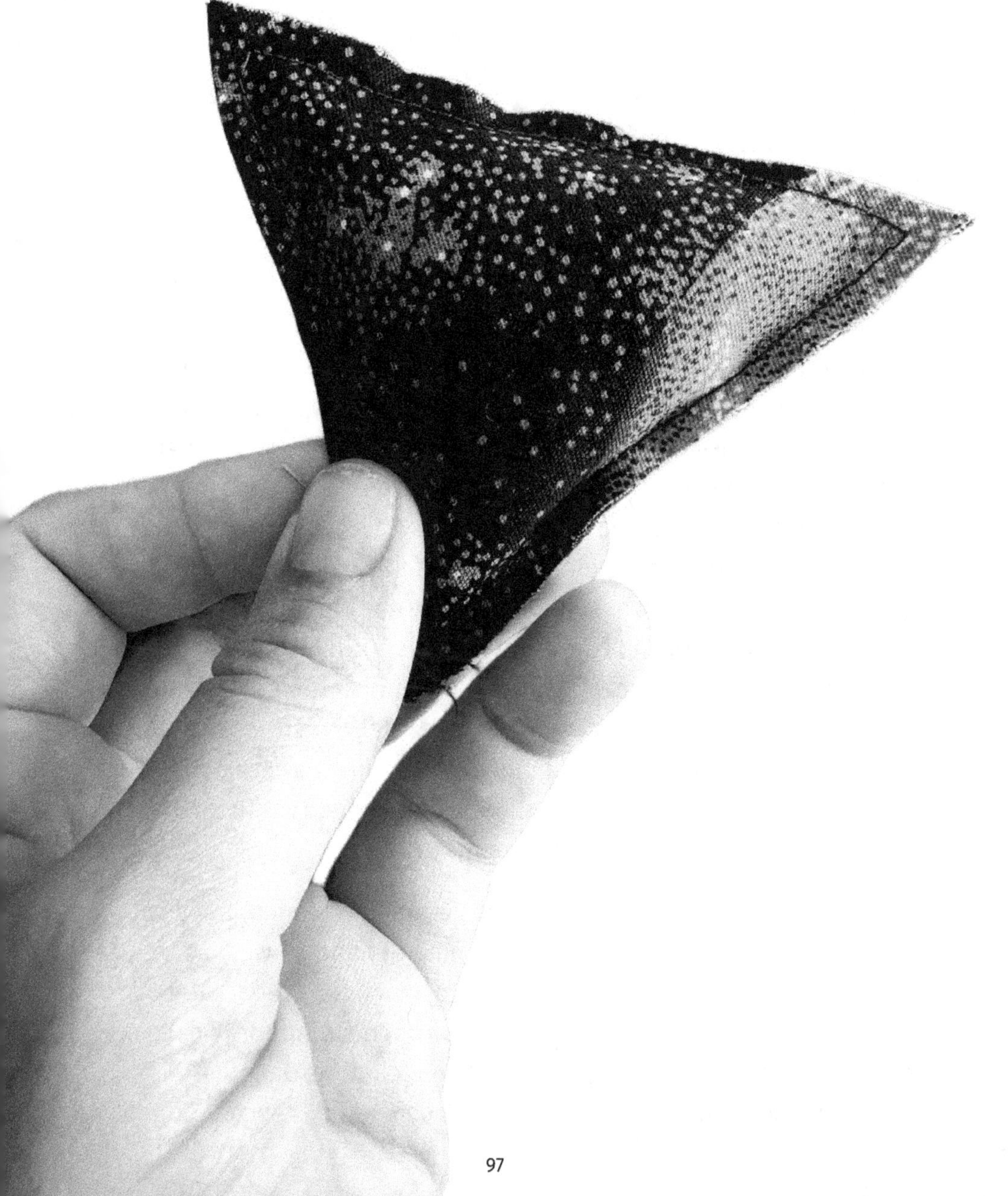

Materials Needed

Fabric squares

Needle, or safety needle

Thread

Polyester stuffing

Binder clips

One of the greatest surprises I've had over the last several years is discovering that my students, as young as 10, love getting to learn how to use my sewing machine and other fiber projects. This type of project has always made me nervous embarking on with such young students, however they are able to make progress in following directions, executive functioning, impulse control, and many others. This project is a great opener to teaching how to safely sew and to safely use a machine that could be intimidating for many adults, even. This project teaches sewing basics and still allows for students to choose their fabric to express a bit of who they are, as they are comfortable. Another benefit is for students who may feel that art is not their forte, this is a utilitarian skill that can be helpful for years to come, even after they finish their education. For ASD students, this type of project can make a lot of sense because as I mentioned before, a lot of my clients love working in three dimensional. Being able to take two flat pieces of fabric and construct them into a 3D object can be very satisfying for students!

This directive can take up to two group sessions when leading it with students. It will depend on student stamina of hand sewing, as well as how quickly students can learn the sewing machine. Prepare to have a backup directive or plenty of options for open studio for two weeks before planning to lead this project. When I lead this directive with high school students, we use a sewing machine and I teach them how to thread the needle, wind the bobbin, and set up the sewing machine program for a straight stitch. I do this method with older students because I have one sewing machine so while I am working with a student to sew their pillow, the other students have to wait for their turn at the machine. This time is set aside for open art studio and in my experience, older students are able to maintain their emotional regulation and patience while waiting for their turn to sew together their pillow. For younger students, we use plastic safety needles and we do each step of it together so that I can have eyes on each student and they can still experience the construction of their pillow from start to finish. I will complete this project and other projects with younger students when I meet individually with them - it really is incredible how quickly they catch on to this type of fiber art!

What I've found works best for machine sewing projects is buying either fabric remnants or felt squares in bulk from your local craft store or Amazon. It is the most budget friendly and offers the most varied choices for students to choose from. For group preparation, the leader can decide if it would be best to have all fabric squares cut down to size before students enter the class or if they will allow students to cut their fabric. There are benefits to both. For cutting the fabric before the group, students can focus on sewing their pillows and learning only that skill. For younger students who will be using a needle and thread, this is likely the best scenario. However, when working with older students you can give them the option to make their pillow any shape they would like. As you can see, I've made triangles and squares, but I've also had students create circles, hearts, and even barbells. This requires students willing to safely use scissors before beginning the sewing, but if that suits your group then it is a great option!

Because there are essentially two options for creating these pillows, I will include group instructions for both the sewing machine and the needle sewing directives. Obviously, this project comes with substantial safety risks, including operating a sewing machine with a sharp needle and the use of scissors. I would not recommend leading this directive with a newer group of students that you have not yet gotten to know in the context of a group setting. In a school, we do have the benefit of having a good amount of information about each students, however even then this is a project I would perhaps save for second semester or even a summer class. If you have a group of students who you feel would benefit from this project but who cannot keep themselves safe, you could have squares pre-cut, have students sit around one table, hand out safety plastic needles (numbered as you would number scissors), and have additional co-leaders or aides assist as you sew together. You will know your students best!

Group Leader Prep For Younger Students Hand Sewing

1. Leader will collect fabric scraps and cut them down to a uniform size. I typically start with a 4x4" square or similar.
2. Collect and number plastic sewing needles for students to use when sewing the fabric together.
3. Make sure you have enough stuffing and thread for each student. When hand sewing, I use embroidery floss with the plastic needle because the eye of the needle is larger than normal.

Group Instructions For Younger Students Hand Sewing

1. Students will watch a demo about a simple running sewing stitch.
2. Once the demo is complete, students will choose two pieces of cut fabric (it can be matching or they can mix their patterns if they choose).
3. Students will receive a plastic needle and a long piece (arms length) of embroidery floss.
4. They will tie a knot on one end of the floss and the other end they will thread through the eye of the needle. I recommend students tying a single knot once the thread is through the eye so that it does not fall out as they sew.
5. Once every student has their fabric squares and their needle threaded, they will use binder clips to attach their two squares of fabric. This will reduce frustration experienced while beginning the initial stitch so that the fabric does not become crooked or fall away from its match.

6. Once fabric is clipped together, the students and group leader will begin sewing a simple running stitch, which is running the needle and thread over and under the fabric so that it forms a tight and secure line. The stitch should start on one corner of the square.

7. Once the thread is almost through the fabric of the first hole, students will tie a knot so that the thread does not pull all the way through the hole.

8. Students will continue this stitch until they reach the end of the first edge. They will then repeat this on the next two edges, until three of the four sides of the square are sewn.

9. At this time, students will take a handful of polyester fluff and stuff it into their pillow pocket. The stuffing should be enough to see the pillow become rounded in the middle, but not too much where the remaining edge will not close.

10. Once the stuffing is in the pillow, students will complete the final edge of the square.

11. Once the final edge is complete, students will tie a knot with the needle so that it does not come unsewn. I recommend students use the remainder of the thread attached to their needle and tie it to the remaining thread that was used to tie the initial knot on the first stitch.

12. Once the sewing is complete, students will safely use scissors (or group leader will use scissors) to cut off any remaining strings left on the pillow.

Modifications/Autism Considerations

1. Students may need a visual print out of each step so that they can follow along with the group leader.

2. Depending on students' fine motor skills, they may need support in threading the needle and tying knots.

3. In addition to the visuals of each step, having a written list of sequential steps that will need to be taken could help students who may have difficulty with executive functioning.

Group Leader Prep For Sewing Machine

1. Leader should collect fabric squares or remnants from a local craft store.
2. Become familiar with your sewing machine so that if troubleshooting is needed, students do not become frustrated with their project being stalled.
3. Make sure polyester fluff is available, as well as scissors for students to make their pillow pattern.
4. Additionally, consider having simple patterns printed off for students to use or refer to as they are cutting their fabric.
5. Because open studio will be occurring simultaneously, ensure there are materials students can independently access as they wait for their turn at the sewing machine.
6. Thread the needle on the sewing machine so that it is ready to go!

Group Instructions For Sewing Machine

1. Group leader will give a demo about the sewing machine and show examples of various pillows students will be able to create.
2. Students will have access to fabric remnants that they may choose from for their pillow. Similar to the other version of this project, they can choose matching sides for their pillow or they can have a mismatched pillow.
3. Students will decide if they want to use a simple shape for their pattern, or if they would like to draw and then cut out a more advanced shape. *Note: encourage students to keep their pillow to around the size of 4x4" even if they are not using a square template for their project.
4. If safe to do so, students will be given scissors to cut their fabric to the shape they would like. If students are creating their own shape, they should use a Sharpie to outline what they will be cutting. This way, if they make a mistake they can correct it without wasting fabric.
5. Once students have drawn and cut out their pillow, they will lay them against one another to ensure that the two sides match up before

they begin sewing. If they are crooked or not aligned, they will make adjustments with their scissors.

6. As each student completes the prep work for their pillow, the group leader will have them walk over with their fabric shapes to the sewing station. When I lead this directive, I usually will set up the sewing machine at my desk so that there is space between the group of students and the individual sewing their pillow.

7. When a student is ready for sewing, the leader will call them over to the sewing machine and they will receive a reiteration of the sewing demo.

8. The leader will then assist the student in placing their fabric under the foot of the machine and then locking it down to secure the fabric.

9. Then the leader and student will lower the needle.

10. Once this occurs, the leader will monitor the fabric near the needle and the foot so that the student is able to safely see the project occur. I have the student in charge of the foot pedal while I guide the fabric under the foot and needle.

11. If a student has experience with a sewing machine, I will have them demonstrate what safety skills are needed and then will allow them to guide the fabric if they are interested.

12. Once the sewing is complete on the sewing machine, we will cut the remaining thread and then the student may take their pillow and return to open studio.

13. This will be repeated until each student has their project completed.

Modifications/Autism Considerations

1. While ASD students are able to pick up this skill readily, a visual guide to the components of a sewing machine, as well as written instructions will be helpful.

2. If students are having difficulty making their own shape, consider having backup squares (as were used with younger students) in case they do not feel comfortable making their own shape or using scissors.

3. When I have led this previously, students became very interested in

then using these skills to create custom plushies or larger sewn items. If this is the case, remind them that to be fair to the rest of their peers, they need to stick to the parameters given. However, if there is time in the student's class schedules, they could set up individual sewing time to work on their larger projects.

Example

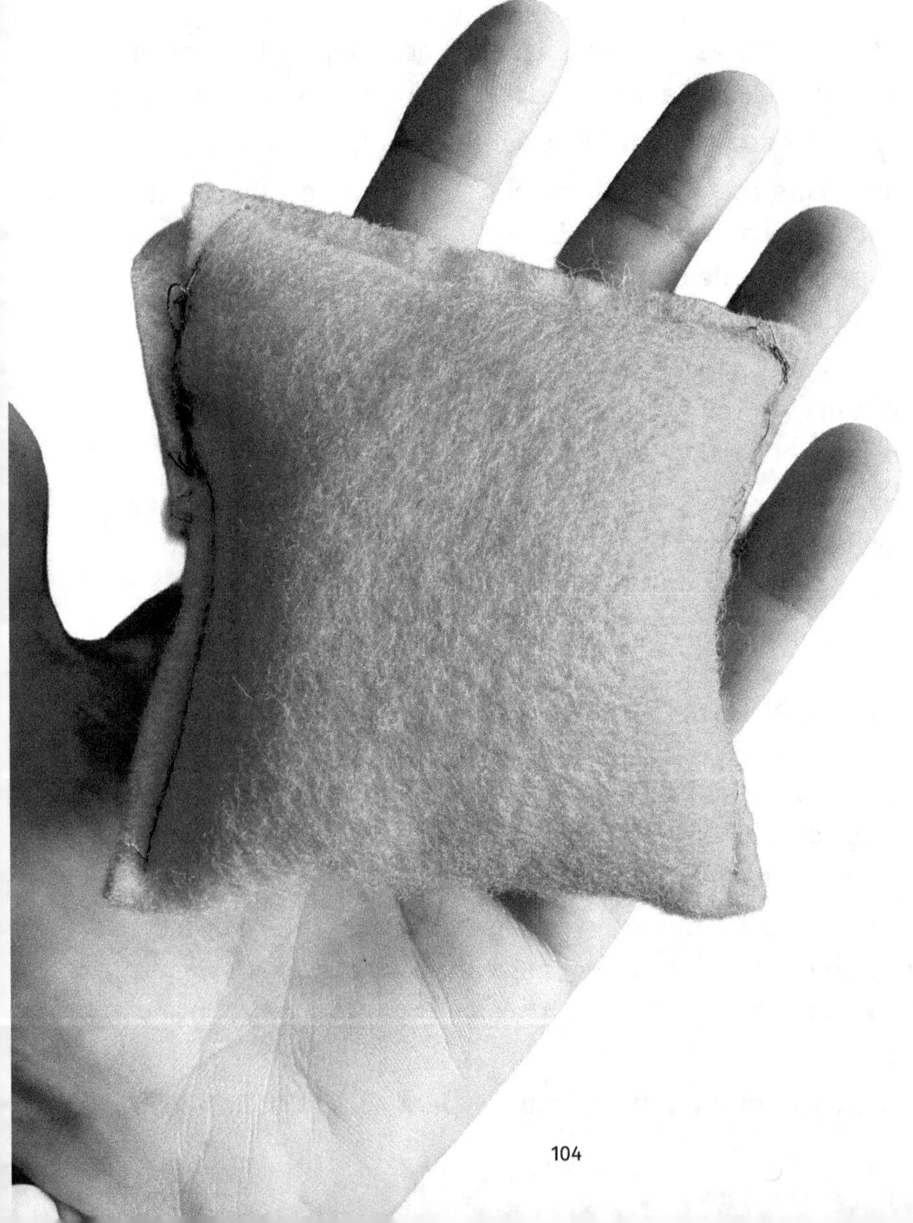

DIRECTIVE 15

Papermaking

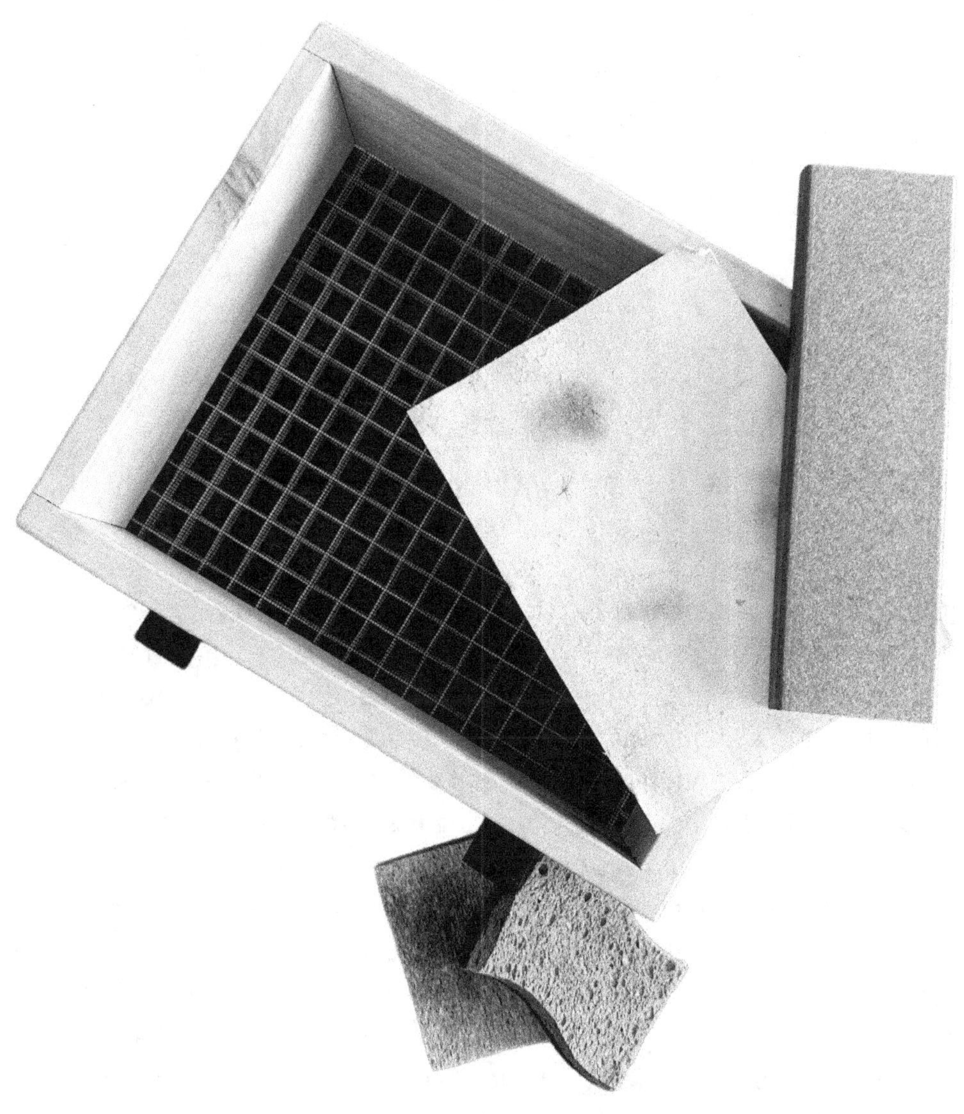

Materials Needed

Paper scraps to turn into paper pulp

Mould and deckle

Blender

Food coloring

Herbs or small flowers/plants

Sponges

Absorbent paper

Shallow bucket for water

Drying rack

Papermaking. I remember my mom making paper with my class when I was in elementary school and from the minute we started that project I loved it. Later when I studied undergrad at the University of Tennessee (Go Vols), I took a papermaking class for a semester and every second of it was so fun. The process involved in each step was so important for the final product, and creating something by hand that most people don't think twice about was a dream come true (I'm a glutton for processes that take a long time and that are old, and this may be why I also love printmaking). But anyway, I digress. Papermaking is full of sensory experiences and getting to employ this with ASD students has been incredible, albeit a bit messy. This project is the last in this book for a reason. It's probably not the one you want to do on the first day of school or with students who are brand new to your group. That being said, I always think that giving kids a way to create something that they probably will not have another chance to make is worth the time and energy that will go into a project such as this.

Creating your own paper can lead down quite the rabbit hole and eventually that paper is used to make books, pull prints, collage, sew into, draw into, etc. etc. I'm somewhere probably ¾ of the way down that rabbit hole, and I've loved every twist and turn. When doing this project with students, opening them up to the possibilities of papermaking, other artists using this process, and the many ways they can expand their own practice with the help of papermaking can motivate ASD students to see the many benefits of papermaking. The benefits of papermaking are many and I've included some of them here. The first benefit I can think of is that it really is an immersive sensory experience that most students enjoy! The pulp has a very interesting feel and there are few rules when it comes to their hands being in the pulp, moving the pulp around, and feeling the pulp with multiple senses. Papermaking is basically like a liquid, moving fidget. Another benefit is that if, as your collecting unwanted artwork over the weeks before to use as the eventual pieces of paper for the paper pulp, it is a great model that even things that we do not like or want can be remade into something beautiful! Another benefit is again, giving students a great opportunity to practice executive functioning, sequential steps, and following directions. Oftentimes, these skills are difficult for students on the spectrum and they can benefit by engaging in projects that give them contained and safe ways to practice these skills.

This project can be completed with groups as young as 10-12, but it will require that you have help from either a co-leader or staff who work with the students (in my case these are program assistants). If students are tearing paper and making the pulp, then it will likely take two art therapy group sessions, with the beginning of a third session so that they can receive their dried paper. While it does take some time to complete this directive, it is worth it for students to discover a new process of artmaking, new materials, and new ways to explore their identity.

As far as physical safety goes, there are no sharp objects involved with this project and no dangerous materials. However, what you will want to ensure is as students are moving around and talking amongst themselves about what steps to do next, some students may find themselves feeling very overloaded with multiple sensory aspects. If they feel flooded with these emotions, then they may become dysregulated or need some time away. It will be important to understand what signs your students display when they begin to feel dysregulated so that you can step in and offer them a break from the room, or a break with a fidget or something similar.

Group Leader Prep

1. Over the weeks leading up to this directive, I recommend collecting paper scraps from other projects or if students state they do not want their artwork to take home or to leave, have them add it to the pile of paper. This will make the day of paper tearing go a lot smoother.

2. When I lead this directive, I tear a lot of the paper beforehand because the stamina for students to continue to tear paper may not last very long. However, I would save some so that they can engage in the sensory aspect of tearing paper, and so they can experience the full process.

3. You will need to fully set up the room before group begins so that there can be order within the chaos of paper making! Make sure you have two tables in the room you will be using.

    - Cover one table with plastic tarp and set out two large rectangular buckets filled at least halfway with water.
    - Next to each of these buckets, place your mould and deckle. It works great if you have two because then two lines of students can use them simultaneously.
    - Set out sponges next to the buckets as well.
    - For Table two, you will also spread out plastic tarp and then either a drying rack, individual plastic trays, or plexiglass should be on top of the tarp.
    - This will be the paper drying station so make sure it's far enough away from the water table to keep the table as neat as possible.
    - Near the drying station, you will need absorbent paper, sponges, and flowers (or other dried natural items).

4. Other items the group leader needs to make sure they have are plastic containers for the paper pulp, aprons, and gloves.

5. If you have never done papermaking, make sure to familiarize yourself with the processes involved.

Group Instructions

1. If paper has not been torn by group leader, students will tear up paper into small inch or smaller size scraps for the paper pulp.

2. Using the 1" paper scraps, put them into your blender until halfway full.

3. Pour warm water into the blender, about a ½ cup at a time. Blend until the water is fully absorbed by paper. Repeat this process until the paper pulp has a consistency of a smoothie (you should not see paper chunks).

4. Transfer the pulp to a plastic container, similar to a to-go soup container.

5. Depending on the size of the class and the number of variations you would prefer for the project (e.g., color, natural items being added, number of pulled sheets), repeat Steps 2 through 4 three to four more times. Keep in mind you can always quickly blend more if needed.

6. At this time, if students wish to dye the paper pulp, they will add three to five drops of food coloring to one plastic container of pulp for a lighter hue, and five to eight drops for a darker hue. Consider having several colors available for students to choose from.

7. Once the pulp is all made and separated into their containers, it is time to begin pulling paper!

8. Students will gather around the table where the large, flat buckets of water are waiting. Consider having two buckets and split the students into two groups.

9. Using the mould and deckle, student will place it into the water so that the water covers just the top of the mesh screen.

10. Then, they will pour one of the paper pulp containers into the mould and use their hand to spread the pulp around. The pulp will mix with the water and begin to spread into the corners and edges of the

mould and deckle.

11. Once paper pulp covers the entire surface of the mesh inside the mould, the student will pull the mould and deckle out of the water and let the water drain from the mould.

12. At this time, the student will carry the mould and deckle to the paper drying station previously set up by group leader. The deckle should be unclasped from the mould so that the mesh remains with the pulp on top of it.

13. Before the next step, the student can return the mould box to the water station so that the next student can begin to repeat steps 9-12.

14. Once the student returns to the drying station, they will use the absorbent paper and place it on top of the paper pulp.

15. Using a sponge, they will press the paper into the pulp to drain any extra water out of the paper pulp.

16. Once complete, they will flip the deckle, or mesh screen, over onto the drying surface.

17. If the paper does not immediately come off of the screen, they will use the sponge to assist the paper pulling away from the mesh. They will press the sponge down across the screen on all sides. This will pull away any extra water and force the paper to fall away from the deckle.

18. Once the paper begins to pull away from the screen, continue to slowly pull away the screen from the paper.

19. At this time if students would like to add any flowers or other natural materials to their paper, they will do so carefully while the paper is still wet. They will gently push the flowers into the surface of the paper, about halfway into the paper.

20. The paper is now ready to dry, and as time allows the student may return to pull another sheet of handmade paper.

21. These steps will be repeated for the group until each student has pulled at least one sheet.

22. The following group session, pass out the paper to the students and allow them an opportunity to see and feel their paper they created!

23. At this time, they can keep the paper as it is, they can cut it so that it has a straight edge, or they can draw back into it with pen, if they would like. You can leave this up to each individual student.

Modifications/Autism Considerations

1. This is clearly a very sensory heavy project. For most students, it will be an experience they enjoy as they get to use their hands and feel the different sensations of the paper pulp. However, some students may have difficulty with getting dirty or feeling the temperature of the water, or the feeling of pulp in general. If this is the case there are a few options.
    - Offer gloves so that their hands do not directly touch the pulp.
    - Provide aprons as well so that they can protect their clothing.
    - If students do not want to touch the pulp at all, consider working in collaboration with them to create their sheet of paper. They can choose the color, amount of paper, and any additions they would like to put into their paper and the group leader can do the physical part of pulling the paper.

2. There is a lot of movement involved at multiple stations for this project and this could feel overwhelming for students so you can allow students multiple breaks and can even have a corner of the room dedicated to students who need to step away from the project.

3. Similar to other projects, including a visual of instructions will be helpful for students who may have difficulty understanding or remembering a list of tasks needed for a project.

Example

Further Research & Reading

American Art Therapy Association
    https://my.arttherapy.org/professional-development/learn-
    ing-and-research

Art Therapy Institute
    https://at-institute.arttherapy.org/

What is Art Therapy
    https://arttherapy.org/what-is-art-therapy/

Contacts for Professional Art Therapists

https://arttherapy.org/art-therapist-locator/

https://atcb.org/find-a-credentialed-art-therapist/

Materials

Basic art supplies that I use I typically will purchase from Amazon or a local craft store, including the sensory items used in Directive 1, as well as markers, colored pencils, etc used throughout this book. For some of the more specific materials I recommend I have listed the places I typically purchase them. This is by no means an exhaustive list but will give a great starting place. It is also worth checking if there are any places in your area that offer free supplies and materials for art therapists and teachers!

Blick Art Materials

- Blick Baby Press
- Book board
- Bone folders
- Mat board
- Papermaking Classroom Kit
- Rubber Brayers
- Water-based relief printmaking ink
- Watercolor paper

Local Craft Store

- Canvas
- Craft supplies (puff balls, foam, etc.)
- Fabric
- Needles, including safety needles
- Polyester stuffing, or filling
- Sewing machine
- Thread

Amazon

- Block printing barens (hand burnishers)
- Foam brushes
- Mini cardboard boxes
- Model Magic
- Perler Beads and accessories
- Pipettes
- Plexiglass sheets
- Styrofoam plates
- Watercolor paints

Art Materials Reference Page

Material	Advantages	Disadvantages
Pencils	Familiar, allows most control, erasable, provides structure	Lack of color, frequent erasing can tear paper, inhibits expression
Crayons	Familiar, continue to use when broken, introduces color with control	Hard to mix colors, can't erase, seen as childish
Colored Pencils	Familiar, allows control, color can help access feelings	Controlled, hard to make strong solid color, breakable
Photo Collage	Easily controlled, stimulates imagination by finding images, combines words and images	Takes time to find and cut images, glue can be messy
Markers/Felt Pens	Familiar, easily available, bright colors, large selection of color, can control amount of emotional expressiveness	Dry out, not erasable, some are not washable
Perler Beads	Controllable, no color mixing, patterns available, safe intro to sculpture, repetition can be regulating	Easy to bump and mess up patterns, requires decent fine motor skills
Oil Pastels	Wide range of colors, moves easy, blendable, kinesthetic/sensory, can cover layers of feelings, wide range of emotional input with some control	Can be messy, sensory component
Model Magic	Range of color, blendable, kinesthetic, can be regulating, can reshape, less need for perfection, easy clean up	Breakable when dry, hard to add fine details
Sculpy	See above, plus greater color selection, easy to take apart and rebuild	Frustration possible until skills are learned, may access strong feelings unexpectedly
Acrylic	Ability to change level of control and layer details, more control than watercolors; Intro to fluid materials	Not washable, can be frustrating to lack control with paintbrush
Wet Clay	Careful consideration for those needing to give up control, can relax need for "talent"	Easily becomes formless, messy, can become "out of control"
Watercolor	Can be liberating, invites colorful expression, can be enhanced with other materials	Difficult to control, inhibits specific expression of image, colors can blend to brown

References

Danieli, Y., Snir, S., Regev, D., & Adoni-Kroyanker, M. (2019). Suitability of the art therapy room and changes in outcome measures in the education system. International Journal of Art Therapy, 24(2), 68–75. https://doi.org/10.1080/17454832.2018.1564778

Durrani, H. (2019). A Case for Art Therapy as a Treatment for Autism Spectrum Disorder. Art Therapy, 36(2), 103–106. https://doi.org/10.1080/07421656.2019.1609326

Hinz, L.D. (2009). Expressive Therapies Continuum: A Framework for Using Art in Therapy. New York, New York: Taylor and Francis Group, LLC.

Monet, C. (1872). Impression, Sunrise. Musée Marmottan Monet.

Pesso-Aviv, T., Regev, D., & Guttmann, J. (2014). The unique therapeutic effect of different art materials on psychological aspects of 7- to 9-year-old children. The Arts in Psychotherapy, 41(3), 293–301. https://doi.org/10.1016/j.aip.2014.04.005

Schweizer, C., Knorth, E. J., van Yperen, T. A., & Spreen, M. (2019). Consensus-based typical elements of art therapy with children with autism spectrum disorders. International Journal of Art Therapy, 24(4), 181–191. https://doi.org/10.1080/17454832.2019.1632364

Schweizer, C., Spreen, M., & Knorth, E. J. (2017). Exploring What Works in Art Therapy With Children With Autism: Tacit Knowledge of Art Therapists. Art Therapy, 34(4), 183–191. https://doi.org/10.1080/07421656.2017.1392760

Van Gogh, V. (1889). Starry night The Museum of Modern Art.

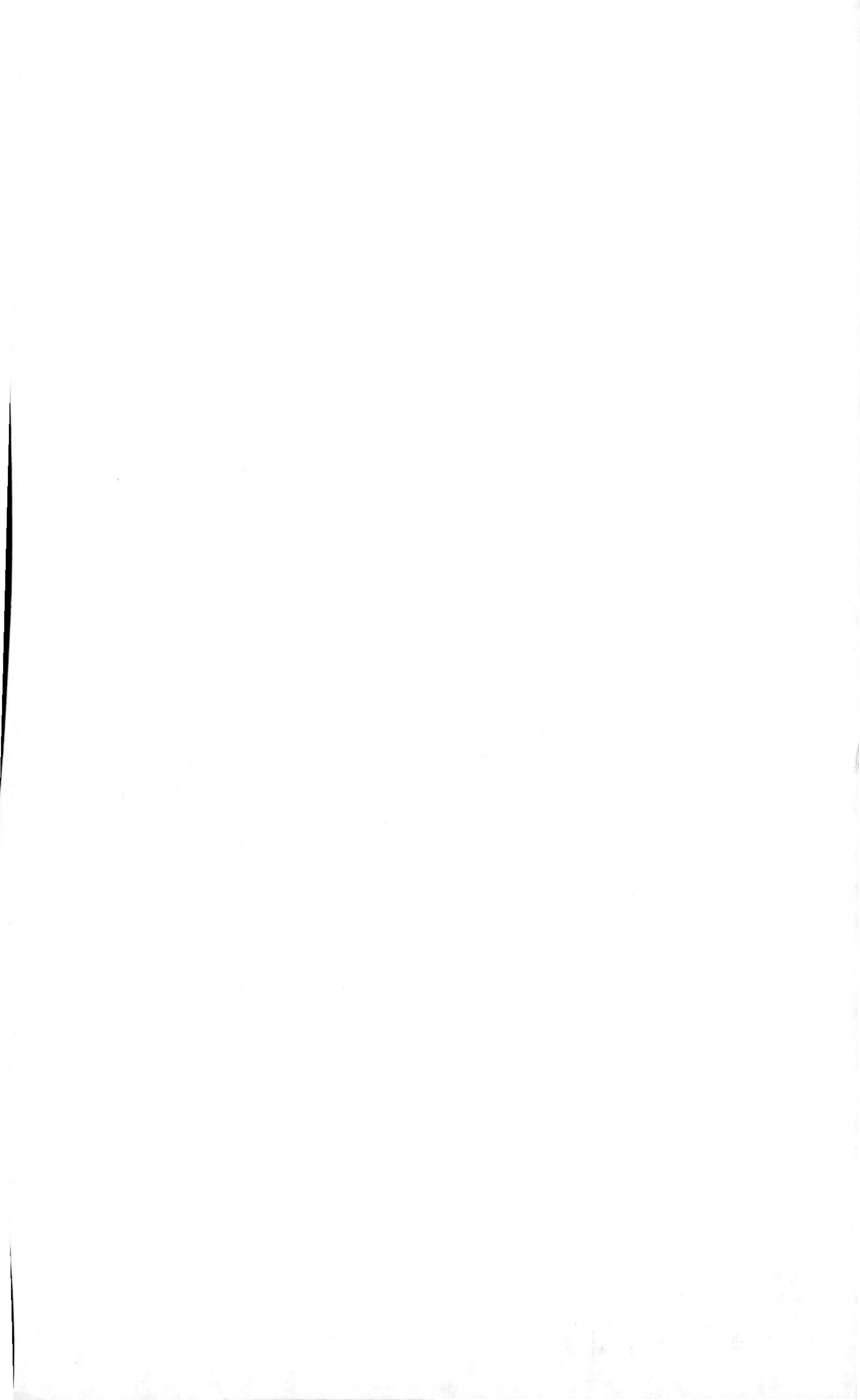